The
Early
Entrepreneur

{ **VIRGIL ADAMS** }

ISBN: 1463556624
ISBN-13: 9781463556624

For my father, a self-made man who
taught me what it is to be an entrepreneur.

Contents

Acknowledgments

Thank you to my wife, Ariel, who has supported me in all my business ventures and created a few of her own as well. She's also given me Logan, Jordan, and Trinity, the future entrepreneurs of our family and the joy of our lives.

Introduction

WHAT WOULD YOU DO?

Picture this: You're 20 years old and have accomplished what most young people in America can only dream of—you've gotten into Harvard University. Once the initial excitement and anxiety of winning admittance wear off, you start settling into your classes. At first, things are overwhelming and awkward; there's so much to learn, everyone is so bright, and you're out on your own for the first time in your life.

By the time you're a junior, you're feeling pretty confident about things; you enjoy the campus, the professors, the classes, and your friends. You're doing well in school and enjoying life. Things are comfortable and the future is bright.

One day, a good friend from high school contacts you and says he wants you to drop out of college to work full-time on a start-up business. He's a couple of years older than you and is working at a company in town. He's a geeky guy that spends all his time working, and thinks he has come across a once-in-a-lifetime opportunity to create a great business. He feels that if you don't seize the chance now, your window of opportunity will be gone, and he can't wait another year for you to graduate; it's either now or never.

What would you do? Would you consider dropping everything you've worked for, only a year from graduating, to strike out with your friend? Could you leave the security that a Harvard degree affords to put in eighteen-hour days laboring for a start-up in a new field of business? What kinds of questions would you ask yourself and your potential business partner?

20/20 HINDSIGHT

What if I told you that the geeky young kid in the example above was Paul Allen, the junior at Harvard was Bill Gates, and the year was 1976? Of course, the company that Gates and Allen founded was Microsoft, which would become one of the largest and most successful corporations of all time.

With the benefit of 20/20 hindsight—knowing today what the outcome of a choice made in the past would be —the decision to drop out and start a company with Paul Allen is a no-brainer. At the time, though, taking the leap to leave Harvard and start a business writing computer code would have been a very difficult thing to do.

Bill Gates saw something back then. He saw the need for an operating system that would make personal computers accessible to the average person, and the opportunity to create that system. He knew he could do it. In fact, he felt sure enough of himself that he was able to turn his back on another opportunity: the chance to graduate from one of the world's most prestigious universities. Not only did he know he could do it, he knew that if he didn't seize the opportunity then and focus on it exclusively, the chance would pass him by.

What is it that drives people like Bill Gates? What allows them to see opportunities that other people can't? What compels them to leave security behind and take risks that most people would feel very uneasy about? Most important, what is it that makes young entrepreneurs succeed?

HOW TO SUCCEED AS AN ENTREPRENEUR

There are no hard-and-fast rules about being an entrepreneur -- a person who starts a business -- but there are many misconceptions about the subject. One purpose of this book is to dispel some of the many myths and misunderstandings about what it means to create your own company.

It might surprise you to know that Bill Gates and Paul Allen didn't follow the prescriptions in this book when they created Microsoft, one of the most successful companies of all time. Larry Page and Sergey Brin probably didn't read any books or follow any formulas before setting up Google while they were still students at Stanford, either. These people didn't spend time making plans, doing market studies, or putting together financial models; they just did it.

We'll never know if Bill Gates could have made Microsoft what it is today if he had stayed at Harvard and joined the company after graduating, but we do know that for every Bill Gates or Sergey Brin, there are millions of Gus Leonards and Chris Harringtons. Who are these guys? They're two of the millions of entrepreneurs who thought they could take the path that Mr. Gates and Mr. Brin did, but who failed spectacularly. You've never heard of them because they vanished with their companies. We live in a country that celebrates success and turns its back on failure. When people like Bill Gates make it, they get so much media coverage that it makes it seem like anyone can replicate their success.

But that's not true. The reality is that business is like swimming. You can be so confident in your abilities that you jump into the deep end right away, or you can approach the task slowly, taking lessons, practicing in the shallow end, and building yourself up for the move to bigger things.

Gates and Brin were two people who jumped in the deep end and managed to survive and thrive. This book will look at when "just doing it" -- just launching a business without putting a lot of work into the planning process -- is the best path to take. For most people, though, jumping into a deep pool without any practice or preparation is more likely to result in drowning than in an effective swimming lesson. For the vast majority of would-be young entrepreneurs, planning and practice are the easiest ways to increase the odds of success.

THIS BOOK IS FOR YOU

This isn't just another book about business or about start-ups. This book is about how to create a company *when you're young*.

Why work for minimum wage doing a menial job at a place you don't like, when you can be the owner of a business, making more money, having more freedom, and doing things your way? There are literally millions of young business owners in this country, each of whom started by asking themselves this question. Many of these people had to set up their companies without much direction or guidance, making costly mistakes along the way. In some cases, these mistakes cost many business owners their companies.

This book is for young people who already know they might want to do something other than work for someone else. This book is for people that believe they have something the world wants, but don't know quite how to package it, deliver it, and charge for it. Whether you're thinking of a babysitting or lawn mowing service for the people in your neighborhood, a web-site-design business that people all over the country might use, or a new product that will revolutionize the world, you'll find that most of the steps involved in setting up a successful business are the same.

YOUNG PEOPLE ARE NATURAL ENTREPRENEURS

People between the ages of twelve and twenty-five have unique abilities, talents, and inspirations that make them specially suited for creating the Teslas and Facebooks of tomorrow, but also have some traits that might lead them to fail or give up prematurely. Young people face challenges that older entrepreneurs don't.

This book looks at the traits that define a successful entrepreneur; that drive a young person to take risks that older people have difficulty understanding; and to succeed where other people fail. It shows you a way of assessing the risks you're taking when you start a business, and how to minimize those risks. It shows you how you can set up and manage a business while still juggling schoolwork, extracurricular activities, and a social life. It explains ways to get around the fact that you might not have any money to start your business or any experience in running a company.

This book will show you what you need to do if you're thinking of being an entrepreneur, whether now or in the future. It will show you steps you need to take to decide on a business, how to launch a company, what work you should do to increase the chance of your firm's success, and even how to exit your business. It will also show you the trade-offs you'll make in choosing an entrepreneurial path versus the more conventional path of working for someone else. The book will point out the hurdles and pitfalls that lie in wait for many entrepreneurs, especially young ones.

If you've picked up this book, there's something different about you -- something within you that says "I can do things better than other people and I don't want someone else getting in my way." This book will show you how to take that motivation and turn it into something real. You'll see that being young is a benefit -- not a drawback --when starting a business, and you will learn how to clear a path to success as an entrepreneur and business owner.

The Sections of this Book

PART 1: WHAT DOES IT MEANS TO BE AN ENTREPRENEUR?

This section answers the question, "Is entrepreneurialism right for me?" We'll look at some of the benefits and drawbacks associated with being an entrepreneur and what makes a good entrepreneur. We'll also help you get in the right frame of mind for launching a business and look at a process for deciding on the type of business that's right for you and that has the best chance of success. We'll also dispel some of the most common myths about entrepreneurs.

PART 2: HOW DO YOU DECIDE ON A BUSINESS?

This section is devoted to outlining the thought processes you should follow before launching a business. It shows you some things to consider in evaluating a potential business idea, including the importance of understanding the industry your company will be in. You'll also see some common mistakes that young entrepreneurs make.

PART 3: HOW DO YOU PLAN THE BUSINESS?

This is the longest section of the book, as it covers the important ground between coming up with a business idea and actually launching a company based on that concept. This section covers the very important—and often neglected—issue of business planning. In it, you'll learn how to make a thorough and convincing business plan, as well as other plans that you should consider as you prepare to launch. You'll also learn about getting funding for your company and how to exit the business.

PART 4: HOW DO YOU LAUNCH THE COMPANY?

In this final section, you'll learn the steps required to register your company and start operations -- all of the steps necessary to make things legal and official. You'll see the importance of keeping your business accounts separate from your personal ones, and how to deal with business failure.

There's a lot of ground to cover, so let's get started.

What It Means to Be an Entrepreneur

Chapter 1:

The Entrepreneurial Mind

BUSINESSPEOPLE, ENTREPRENEURS, AND WHERE YOU FIT IN

The idea of starting a company might seem like a difficult, intimidating, and complicated endeavor to most young people. Or you may think that the idea of starting a formal business is unnecessary. Why go to the trouble?

You will soon see that setting up a company can be easy, inexpensive, and rewarding on many levels.

ARE YOU A BUSINESSPERSON?

If you're like most young people, you probably answered "no" to this question. Let's ask the question in a different way: have you ever conducted business?

You might have a different answer to this question. You see, a business is simply something that provides goods or services to others. That can mean anything from babysitting to running a billion-dollar corporation or local nonprofit organization. A businessperson is anyone who has provided a product or service to others.

So, are you a businessperson? You probably are, or easily could be.

There's a difference, though, between a businessperson and an entrepreneur. The difference is similar to that between the typical working-class person and the typical wealthy person.

It's said that people who aren't rich work for their money, while people who are rich make their money work for them. The difference between a typical businessperson and the typical entrepreneur is how the person approaches the goods or services they're providing. The businessperson might not see the potential in what they're doing, and can't get excited about it. The entrepreneur, on the other hand, can see that what they're doing could lead them to riches if they just change their approach a bit.

Let's take the job of babysitting for a neighbor as an example of the typical person's mind-set compared to that of an entrepreneur.

THE BABYSITTER VS. THE ENTREPRENEUR

The typical babysitter sees his or her job as one of selling time. To illustrate what this means – and why it's not the best way to make money – we'll use the example of Jenny the babysitter.

A neighbor might contact Jenny and ask if she can look after some kids on Saturday night. Jenny agrees to watch the kids for three hours at a rate of ten dollars per hour. In other words, she engages in a business transaction in which the customer buys three hours of her time for thirty dollars.

Here are some problems with the approach that Jenny is taking to her babysitting job (if she does want to turn it into something much bigger, that is):

1. The babysitter is reliant upon someone seeking her services. She's not actively trying to find customers; if someone doesn't contact her looking for a sitter next weekend, she'll have no income. She might see this job as a "one-time" event and not look beyond that.

2. The babysitter could be taking on risks that she's not aware of. For example, suppose one of the kids hurts himself while

Jenny is on the phone talking with a friend. Could she be sued by the child's parents for negligence? Could the babysitter's parents and their assets be at risk if the babysitter doesn't have any assets herself?

3. Jenny isn't delivering anything of unique value. Yes, she's watching over the kids and giving the customer peace of mind, but couldn't *any* responsible teenager do that? The babysitter is easily replaceable.

4. Perhaps most important, Jenny has no way to "scale up" her business – to grow it exponentially. (We'll look at what that means later in this book.).

Now, let's look at how an entrepreneur would approach the job of babysitting.

The entrepreneur doesn't want to just sell her time, as she realizes that time is a very limited commodity (we'll look at the importance of time in a moment). She doesn't want to do what any other teenager could; she wants to offer a service that people would be willing to pay more for and that others can't duplicate easily. The entrepreneur-sitter wants to engage not simply in one transaction, but a stream of them. She realizes that she cannot sit back and hope for customers to call her; she will have to drum up business proactively. Finally, she understands that she needs to be able to scale her business up.

Why does she think this way? She might take this approach because she understands the basic math behind the "traditional" route and the entrepreneur route:

A traditional babysitter might be able to make $10 per hour. What's the most she could possibly make? If she were able to work twenty-four hours a day, seven days a week, thirty days a month (which is highly unlikely of course) she'd make $240/day, $1,680/week, or $6,720 per month.

That's the absolute limit to what she could make. Even if she managed to raise her price by $1/hour without losing any business, she would only make an additional $24/day or about $750/month.

By contrast, let's look at the entrepreneur:

The entrepreneur realizes that there is a limit to how many hours she can sell or how much she can charge per hour, so she takes a very different approach: she decides to create a business that finds people who need babysitters and matches them with high school students who are able to babysit.

She forms a company to protect herself from liabilities such as unsatisfied customers suing her. She provides some training for her employees, and guarantees a higher level of care than one could expect from calling just any teenager. She advertises her business, and a friend creates a web site and app that allows customers to book sitters online or through an app on their phone.

She charges $12.50 per hour to dispatch a trained babysitter to the customer. From this, she pays her sitter $10 and keeps $2.50 for herself. The sitter is happy with this arrangement since she gets the $10/hour she wants, and the customer is willing to pay the extra $2.50/hour because they are getting a trained sitter -- someone who has taken a child first-aid course and CPR training, who has been screened by a company and who follows the company's policy of not making personal phone calls during the work hours, and who reads to the kids at bedtime.

Of course, making $2.50 per hour for sending a babysitter to someone's house is a lot less than the $10 she would get from sitting herself; that's where the "scalability" of the business comes into play. If the entrepreneur is doing the babysitting herself, she can make only $10/hour. If she can run a sitter-dispatching service, though, she gets $2.50 per hour per babysitter, and could potentially manage a very large pool of sitters. On any given Saturday night, she might dispatch fifty sitters. Here, the entrepreneur would then be making $125 per hour for her services.

What's the most the entrepreneur could make from her babysitter-dispatch service? Theoretically, it's nearly unlimited.

The entrepreneur can set up a company, make ten times or more per hour than the babysitter, take less risk (of being sued, for example), and earn money while sitting at home and letting her employees do the "real work." Does that sound appealing to you?

The Difference Between the Entrepreneur and the Average Babysitter

The Traditional Babysitter...

	The Traditional Babysitter
How He/She Works	Uses their time; tries to find people who will pay by the hour for sitting services. **Works Hard.**
How to Grow the Business (i.e. "Scalability")	Difficult to grow the business, as the number of hours available to the sitter are limited. **Hard to Scale.**
How to Find Customers	**Usually reactive:** responds to requests from personal network for sitting services
Risks	**High:** the typical sitter has no special insurance, contracts, or any other way to limit personal liability
Opportunities	Usually can't grow beyond a small size, and hard to continue when there are big changes (i.e. moving to a new town, going to college) in the sitter's life

...and The Babysitter-Entrepreneur

	The Babysitter-Entrepreneur
How He/She Works	Uses their brain, not their time: finds sitters and matches them with customers, taking a cut for the service. **Works Smart.**
How to Grow the Business (i.e. "Scalability")	Easy to grow the business: simply a matter of finding more sitters and more customers. **Easy to Scale.**
How to Find Customers	**Proactive**: the entrepreneur actively seeks out customers, advertising to find both sitters and people who need them
Risks	**Low**: has a business structure that limits liability; may have special insurance and contracts
Opportunities	If the service is virtual (with most business conducted on-line), the business can be maintained even if the founder moves or goes to college

The lesson here: time is a precious resource. Time is one of those rare things that, once used, can never be regained. When you're young, time is on your side; you have a lot more time to create and build something than a middle-aged person does. Don't squander your time by selling it at a low price; find a way to get the most money possible from the least amount of time. That's what successful entrepreneurs do, and what you can learn to do also.

Chapter 2:

Understanding Entrepreneurialism

The word "entrepreneur" comes from the French verb "*entre-prendre*," meaning "to do" or "to undertake." An entrepreneur is someone who "does"; someone who acts. Generally, this means putting the time, energy, and money into starting up a business, and being willing to take the risks that come along with it. Where most people see challenges and risks, entrepreneurs see opportunities. Where most people complain about problems, entrepreneurs create solutions.

THE IMPORTANCE OF ENTREPRENEURS

How many companies do you think there are in America? Ten thousand? A hundred thousand? A million? In fact, the Small Business Administration estimates that there are nearly 30 million different companies in the United States. Over 20 million of these companies don't have any employees at all -- they're sole proprietorships, owned and operated entirely by one person, the founder of the company.

Small businesses are the lifeblood of the U.S. economy. According to the Small Business Administration, nearly two-thirds of all new jobs created since 1993 have come from small businesses, and over half of these businesses are run from home!

We're all very fortunate to live in a country that encourages the creation and growth of new companies: about one in ten working people is self-employed or works for a small business, and the process of opening one's own company is relatively easy. In fact, there are government agencies that exist solely to help small companies, tax benefits available for start-ups, and not many federal regulations to deal with in starting a business or keeping it going.

WHO CAN BE AN ENTREPRENEUR?

Anyone can be an entrepreneur. You can have a criminal record and start a company. You could have immigrated to this country a month ago and still be able to start up a business. You can be twelve years old with no money in the bank and just a good idea, and you can still set up a company to sell the product or service that's in your head.

You don't have to be old to create a business: Google, Facebook, and Dell are all examples of companies that were started by students. You don't need a lot of money, either: Microsoft, Nike, Domino's Pizza, Hewlett-Packard, and Eastman Kodak are all examples of companies that were started with ten thousand dollars or less. Don't think that setting up a business is an intimidating task that requires a lot of work, money, and special talent: any U.S. citizen or legal immigrant can start a company in this country.

The question "Who can be an entrepreneur?" wasn't really a fair one, though, was it? If I asked, "Who can play golf?" and you answered "Anyone," you'd be technically right— almost anyone can pick up a club and hit a ball. But the real question should be, "Who can play golf *well*?" Just about anyone can start a company, but being a successful entrepreneur requires a particular type of person, a lot of hard work, and a good measure of luck.

Many people think that today's entrepreneurs were always entrepreneurs, and that they were born with some "entrepreneur gene" that directed them into starting up companies from an early age. In reality, many successful entrepreneurs worked for large corporations for many years, gaining experience, saving money, testing ideas, and making business contacts before venturing off on their own. Later, we'll look at some of the trade-offs that come with being your own boss versus working for someone else.

Entrepreneurs hold a special place in this country. Some of the most important businesspeople that ever lived -- George Washington, Thomas Edison, Dale Carnegie, J.D. Rockefeller, and Warren Buffet -- were or are entrepreneurs. Just about every large corporation you see today was at one time nothing more than an idea in some entrepreneur's mind.

We'll look at a few of the common entrepreneurial myths throughout this section, and this brings us to the first one.

MYTH #1: You need money, special skills, or connections to be an entrepreneur.

REALITY: Anyone can be an entrepreneur; you don't need anything but the right frame of mind.

Why Do People Do It?

There are many different reasons that compel people to become entrepreneurs. For many young people, the key reason is that they have to: many states don't allow people under the age of fourteen to work for someone else. You can form your own business and make your own money when you're twelve or thirteen, but in most places you can't earn money working at McDonald's or Starbucks at that age.

In a weak economy, many people decide to set up their own business because that's their only option for working. The job market might be so bad that they have a better chance of making a living by running their own auto-body shop than by hoping to be hired by another shop when "no one's hiring." Entrepreneurs are people who make their own opportunities, rather than hoping that someone else will create an opportunity for them.

Some people start their own business as a source of additional income. They might have a full-time job and do not want to leave the security and income that it provides, yet they are able to run a business in their free time.

Others might start a company because they've gotten tired of working for someone else. They might resent someone else taking the credit for the work they've done, or getting only a sliver of the money they make for the company. Maybe they believe they're not treated properly in the company, or don't have the same opportunity that others in the company do (perhaps because of their race, sex, background, or other reason).

Some people start businesses out of charity, some out of self-interest, some out of fear ("if I don't act now, I'll never have a chance like this again"), some in search of freedom, and some because they have no other choice. In short, you can find a lot of reasons behind why people become entrepreneurs.

Unfortunately, many people who set up businesses don't know what they're getting themselves into. They don't do the proper planning, don't have realistic expectations, or can't convince others that the idea they believe in so strongly is actually a good one (that deserves, say, a loan from a bank).

Reasons for Being an Entrepreneur

Why Would Someone Become an Entrepreneur?
Ambition (fame, fortune, dreams)
Freedom, individuality, non-conformity
Frustration with corporate environment
Necessity (can't get a corporate job)
Passion (can be a part-time passion)
Fear (worried that you won't be successful any other way)
Charity (believe it's the best way to help society)
DNA (it's in your blood)
Stupidity (you harbor misconceptions about entrepreneurship)
Because they can

> **MYTH #2:** Entrepreneurs are born with a gene that compels them to start businesses when they're young.
>
> ---
>
> **REALITY:** Many entrepreneurs discover their calling only after years of going the "corporate route."

WHAT ARE THE TRADE-OFFS TO BEING AN ENTREPRENEUR?

Many people think only about the glamorous side of being an entrepreneur, imagining the business owner sitting in a nice office with the title of "president" and lots of people working for him or her. That's rarely the reality, even for very successful business owners; for most start-ups, that image couldn't be further from the truth.

Every choice comes with trade-offs, and the choice to start a business is no different. For the entrepreneur that leaves a corporate job to start a company of her own, the trade-offs can be dramatic. For the entrepreneur who decides to bypass the corporate route altogether and start a company right after he or she finishes school (or, in many cases, while still in school), the trade-offs could be far too risky.

Let's talk about money first: How much can an entrepreneur make? That depends on so many different factors that it's impossible to generalize. What can be said with certainty, though, is that the image of an entrepreneur as a business tycoon or young and fabulously wealthy is accurate only for a very small minority of business owners. For every Mark Zuckerberg (the founder of Facebook), there are millions of people who tried and failed, or are still struggling.

Even if you establish a business that covers your expenses, pays you a decent wage, and leaves something left over (a profit) to reinvest in the business and allow it to grow, you'll find that your paycheck can vary greatly from one month to another. With a safe corporate job, you know what you'll make in a given year, and what to expect in your paycheck each pay period. For an entrepreneur, there can be months of either paying oneself nothing, or paying just what's "left over" from operating the business.

Likewise, the ideal of the business owner that doesn't have anyone to report to—that can tell his secretary that he's leaving early to play golf or go to his kid's school play—is something that most business owners can only fantasize about. While you may not have a boss telling you that a project is due tomorrow morning, meaning that you'll have to be at the office until midnight or later, you'll probably have people that are even more demanding: customers. A customer might call you on Friday night and threaten to cancel their account if a problem with something you sold them isn't fixed by Monday. Good-bye, weekend!

Or it could be suppliers that cause the headache. Suppose you start a business organizing kids' birthday parties (we'll come back to this idea in greater detail later). An hour before a big event your bakery tells you they had a problem and can't have the cake ready, and your entertainment—your cousin, who was set to do magic tricks for the kids—finds out his car's broken down and he's going to have to cancel his appearance.

Other benefits, such as health care, paid vacations, paid overtime, retirement savings, and many others are standard fare for a corporate job, but something the budding entrepreneur can only dream about. If you want health care, you're going to pay for it out of your own pocket, or rather your own company's pocket. A vacation? Maybe if you combine it with meeting clients at a trade show or conference. Paid overtime? Now you're making me laugh.

Why, then, with all the benefits that come with working for a good, solid company would someone take the leap and launch their own business? Are all entrepreneurs nuts?

Being Your Own Boss vs. Working for Someone Else: A Comparison

The Entrepreneur...

	Entrepreneur
Money	Can range from negative (you're spendnig more than you're earning) to massive. Can also vary by month, with some lean months and some fat ones.
Job Security	None. You can call yourself the president of Bob, Incorporated, but if you don't have customers, you don't have a job.
Benefits	Varies. You might have more freedom and flexibility (if you want to take Wed. afternoon off, you can), but you generally give up most of the perks that come with working for larger, more established firms.
Time, Stress	Most entrepreneurs live and breathe their companies. There is no "me" time; there's only time for the company. Stress levels can be much higher when your rent payment depends on a customer paying you on time.
Other Risks	You risk your credit, your reputation, your pride; in some cases, the business consumes so much of the founder's time or creates so many problems that family or health problems occur
Other Rewards	Self-fulfillment Sense of accomplishment Freedom

...and The Corporate Employee

	A Corporate Job
Money	Varies, but at least it's stable.
Job Security	Good. Although companies can downsize or let people go, for the most part companies invest in their people, and want to keep them around.
Benefits	Good. Health insurance, retirement savings plans, paid vacation, travel budgets and other benefits.
Time, Stress	With many jobs, your time's not your own -- you might need to stay late or come in on a weekend to get your job done. Still, you probably aren't thinking about the company at all hours of the day and night. Stress is less.
Other Risks	For the most part, the company's "got your back". If you're a valuable employee to the company, you'll be treated well and risks are low
Other Rewards	Predictability Feeling of belonging to a bigger group Peace of mind

My dad's favorite joke (I know it's his favorite because he tells it to me every time I see him) illustrates why many people try to start a business, despite the risks:

Every night before bed, a man prays to God: "Please, Lord, let me win the lottery." Every day, the man is disappointed. Still, he keeps trying: "Please, God, let me win the lottery." Finally, after many years of praying, the man says his prayers and is getting ready for bed. Lightning flashes, thunder erupts, and the man hears the voice of God: "Larry, meet me halfway—at least buy a ticket."

That's the reason that many people pursue the entrepreneurial dream: even if they have no false impressions of what being one's own boss is like and even if they know the trade-offs they face and the sacrifices they will need to make by starting their own company, they know that there's no way to win the "lottery of life" if they don't at least buy a ticket. They can't live with the prospect of not *trying* to turn their idea into a successful business.

The life of an entrepreneur can be very stressful, challenging and hard, but it can also be extremely fulfilling. It can teach you the skills to get a great corporate job later in life, or it can be a wonderful exit from the corporate rat race. Being an entrepreneur, in many ways, is like having a child: it's not for everyone; it comes with great responsibilities; it takes a lot of effort; but it can be more rewarding than anything else you do in your lifetime.

Special Trade-offs for Younger People

If you're still in school and are thinking of running a company before you graduate, you need to consider trade-offs that most entrepreneurs don't: the impact on your grades, your social life, and your stress levels.

There's another trade-off that young people in particular should consider: opportunity costs. Most people think that a "cost" is something measured in dollars, but that's not always the case. An opportunity cost is what you sacrifice in order to do something. For example, if you have a choice of going to the movies with your friends Friday night or working on a paper that's due Monday, then the cost of staying home to work on your paper is the lost enjoyment of hanging out with your friends.

Every decision carries opportunity costs, and the decision to set up and run a business can come with seemingly endless ones. You might have to spend so much time on the business that you miss out on a lot of enjoyable and important things. Running a business when you're in high school or college is a great experience and can be a lot of fun, but it could interfere with your grades, chance to play sports or go to dances, or just enjoy a special time of your life. Real success is about finding and maintaining a healthy balance in life, and that means knowing when the opportunity costs for doing one thing and not another are too high. It means being able to prioritize.

Having a business can mean having something that knows no boundaries; it can intrude on every aspect of your life if you let it. Something you should do if you're going to set up and run a business while keeping up with your schoolwork and maintaining some kind of social life is create "fences" around your non-business life.

Fences are borders. They're a way to partition off things so that your customers' calls don't spill over into your night at the prom or your time studying for finals. You can create one fence by setting up a business phone number and keeping business hours. You might have a voice mail on your business phone that instructs people on how to reach you in the event of an emergency, but otherwise you'll be erecting a barrier between your customers and your private life. You should also try to give yourself breaks. For example, you could pay your little sister to take any calls or run the business each Friday night, so that you can go out and have a good time (with the expectation, of course, that you'll be getting back to anyone that called first thing Saturday or Monday morning).

When I was in high school, I ran a mail-order comic book business from my parents' house. I had a separate business line, and would make and return calls every day from 3:30–5:00 p.m. After dinner, I had to finish all my homework before getting back on the phone or packing comic books to mail the next day. As long as I prioritized my homework, my parents didn't give me any flak about the time I spent working on my business. Likewise, I knew that they could shut me down if I didn't do my schoolwork, so that always came first.

Whether the benefits of being an entrepreneur outweigh the drawbacks is something only you can decide, but the important thing to remember is that most entrepreneurs work harder, make less, enjoy less freedom, and have more stress than the person who gets a job at a big company. Don't harbor any glamorous illusions of what being a business owner is like. If you know what you're getting yourself into, you'll be better prepared for challenges when they arise.

MYTH #3: Owning a business is glamorous.

REALITY: Owning a business is hard work, with long hours, lots of stress, and a ton of struggle.

WHAT DOES IT TAKE TO BE A SUCCESSFUL ENTREPRENEUR?

There are a number of traits that most successful entrepreneurs share. Here's a partial list, in no particular order.

What Entrepreneurs are Like

Characteristics, Traits and Aptitudes of Successful Entrepreneurs
Entrepreneurs are:
• Hard workers
• Organized
• People who understand the big picture, but also know which details are important to follow (they know a few things very well, and a number of other things reasonably well)
• Able to take risks without second guessing themselves
• Able to sacrifice for what they believe in
• Able to handle rejection and failure
• Confident
• Committed
• Able to win the support of others; able to manage teams and win respect of team members
• Decisive and able to make tough decisions
• Flexible, with the ability to adapt
• Able to prioritize
• Able to delegate responsibility
• Passionate
• Optimistic
• Disciplined
• Driven
• Creative
• Able to deal with pressure in a positive way
• Able to plan and prepare well
• Able to set goals and track progress

You don't need to have all of the traits and abilities in the list above to be a successful entrepreneur, but you won't find a lot of successful entrepreneurs that don't have many of these characteristics and talents.

The traits in the list above are necessities. Again, you don't have to possess them all, but the more items on that list you have, the better your chances of success are.

In addition to the list of necessities are "assets": things that might not be critical, but which can give you an edge over others. One asset is age. A young person has many natural advantages when it comes to opening a business. For example, young people are better suited to taking risks. That's something we'll examine next.

The Early Entrepreneur

WHAT IS YOUR RISK TOLERANCE?

> **MYTH #4:** Being successful means taking big risks.
>
> ---
>
> **REALITY:** Success is about defense as well as offense; it's about minimizing risk, not just maximizing opportunity.

This is one of the most common myths about starting a business. Being a successful entrepreneur isn't about taking risks; it's about avoiding or minimizing them without reducing opportunities. There's no way to eliminate risk entirely, but the more risks you can eliminate, the more you're able to focus on achieving your goals. Planning helps you identify and side-step many of the risks that other, less prepared businesspeople exhaust themselves wrestling with.

Of course, in order to control risk, you need to understand what it is. Many people think that risk is just the chance of something bad happening. If I told you there was only a one percent chance of something happening, would you say the risk was low? Most people would say "yes." Now, what if I told you that there was a one percent chance of a nuclear bomb going off in San Francisco on Saturday, killing everyone within twenty miles of the city? Would you still think the risk was negligible?

Risk isn't just the chance of something bad happening, but also the severity of the outcome. A small chance of a terrible outcome can be as risky as a big chance of a not-so-bad outcome.

How to Assess Risk: Expected Returns Analysis

Suppose you ride your bike without a helmet and I told you that there's a two percent chance that you'll fall off your bike and scrape your hands or knees. You might say that's an acceptable risk—a low chance of a not-so-bad outcome. But then, what if I told you that if you did fall off your bike, there was also a ten percent chance that you would hit your head and do irreversible brain damage to yourself? You might think that's not an acceptable risk because even though the chance of it happening is low, the outcome is terrible, and you'd decide to wear your helmet when you rode your bike.

This is the concept of Expected Returns. An Expected Return (ER) is the chance of something happening multiplied by the outcome of the event. Sometimes, there can be many expected returns to the same event, but you can add all of them together to come up with the total ER.

For example, we could flip a coin — if it lands heads up, you get a dollar; if it's tails, you give me a dollar. Here's the expected return of that game:

In this case, you'd say the game is pointless, based on the idea that if we played the game one million times, we'd probably both break even and have wasted a lot of time.

This coin toss example might seem simple and not applicable to real life, so let's apply the concept to a more complicated, real-life decision you might face.

Let's say you're considering starting a company for $1,000. The business has a small chance of being a big success and making a lot of money, but a large chance of being a failure and costing your entire $1,000 investment. Should you put your savings into starting this business?

The first thing to do is to list the possible outcomes for your business ("big success", "small success", "break even", and

A Coin-Flip Game

What is a 50% chance of winning $1.00 worth?

Probability of Winning		50%
Payout if You Win	$	1.00
Expected Return of Winning	$	0.50

(The Equation: Probability x Payout = Expected Return)

What is a 50% chance of losing $1.00 worth?

Probability of Losing		50%
Payout if You Lose	$	(1.00)
Value of the Opportunity	$	(0.50)

(The Equation: Probability x Payout = Expected Return)

What is the Total Expected Return of This Game?

Probability of Winning		50%
Payout if You Win	$	1.00
Expected Return of Winning (A)	$	0.50
Probability of Losing		50%
Payout if You Lose	$	(1.00)
Expected Return of Losing (B)	$	(0.50)
Total Expected Return (A+B)	Zero	

"failure", for example) and what you think the probability of each outcome is. Next, you list the "payoff" under each outcome. For example, if your business is a big success, your $1,000 investment will grow to be worth $10,000. If you multiply the probability of the outcome by the payoff, you get the Expected Return of the business. Add up all the Expected Returns for the total Expected Return.

Should you start the business? Here's what the ER calculation looks like:

An Expected Return Analysis

Outcome	Probability	Payoff	Exp. Return
Big Success	5%	$ 10,000	$ 500
Small Success	10%	$ 5,000	$ 500
Break-Even	30%	$ 1,000	$ 300
Failure	30%	$ (500)	$ (150)
Big Failure	25%	$ (1,000)	$ (250)
Total Expected Return	**100%**		**$ 900**

Total Expected Return on Investment	$	900
Total Investment Cost	$	1,000
Is the Expected Return Greater than the Cost?		No

Given these probabilities and outcomes, you would be expected to get back $900 from the $1000 you put in. Considering all the possibilities, you'd be expected to lose $100. In other words, even though there is a small chance of making a lot of money, this isn't a good investment overall.

Now, it's natural to say, "Wait—only one outcome is possible, and if the outcome that actually comes about is the "Big Success", then you've got $10,000. It's not possible that all of the outcomes happen, so why would you count all of them?" This is true, but you never know in advance what the outcome is going to be. You might say that the odds are sixty percent that the business will be a failure, but there's also a smaller chance you could do all right. When you don't know for certain which outcome will come about, you have to weigh all the possibilities.

You'll find that expected return analysis can be used to evaluate all kinds of financial decisions, from whether to buy an extended warranty on a product to what you should pay for car insurance.

Chapter 3:

The Benefits and Drawbacks of Starting Young

THE BENEFITS OF YOUTH

How many times does an adult assume the position of the wise and experienced person bestowing wisdom to the youngster when speaking about something serious? You might think that I'm going to tell you that being older means being wiser, having more experience, or being better prepared to be a successful entrepreneur. That's not the case.

The problem is that young people are told so often what they *can't* do that they tend to forget what they *can* do. You hear so much about how you're "too young" to do certain things that you start to believe that your age is a liability. "I can't wait until I'm older so I can do what I want to do," you say. Don't let other people create these types of limitations for you.

There are many great advantages that young people have over older people when it comes to starting companies. It just takes a change of perspective.

Rather than look at your age as a problem ("I'm too young to have had any experience or saved any money"), turn that "problem" into an opportunity. Instead of thinking of the things you're "too young for" when it comes to money, can you think of things that you're young enough to be? Can you think of ways that your age can be a great asset when it comes to being an entrepreneur?

One advantage to being young is that you have incredible energy, passion, impatience, intolerance, and time on your hands.

"Wait a minute," you might be thinking. "Did you just say that impatience, intolerance, and too much time were good things?"

Yes, I did. Jim Morrison, the lead singer of the Doors said it best in one of his songs: "We want the world and we want it now." That's as good a statement of the visions and ambitions of young people as I've ever heard. Impatience and intolerance may sound like bad things, but they're behind some of the greatest revolutions in history. Old people grow complacent and invested in the "status quo." They are used to things taking time, and they think it's only natural that problems take a long time to solve -- they have to study them, listen to everyone's opinions, make compromises, broker deals, and take many other steps before coming up with a solution.

Young people, on the other hand, aren't so patient. They haven't been trained to sit on their hands and wait. They want it and they want it now! If they see a problem, they want a solution yesterday. They act first and think later. The next time you see a revolution somewhere in the world televised on the evening news, look who's out on the front lines of that movement: I can almost guarantee it won't be a bunch of people in suits with gray hair. More likely, the people will be young; people who can't wait the two, three, or more years until the next election, or won't tolerate another day of the rule of an incompetent leader. Young people create change because they get fed up with the status quo. The same attitudes that topple governments also create great businesses. The world is changing at a faster pace than ever before. Young people are used to speed like that; old people find it frightening.

Another benefit is that you're young enough to be able to bounce back from setbacks. This allows you to take risks that older people can't or shouldn't.

Suppose you were a middle-aged person working at a large company. You have a great idea for a business, and believe that if you don't act now you'll never have another opportunity like this again. Still, you have a cushy job and might be up for a promotion; you have a big mortgage and two kids in college. You're worried about what would happen if you left your job to start a company that failed. You know how hard it is for a middle-aged person to get back onto the corporate track once they leave. You decide not to take the chance, as you have too much to lose. You stay in the company until you retire, always wondering what could have been.

You -- the young person -- on the other hand, has your whole life ahead of you. If you take a risk and your company fails, you have the rest of your working life to make up for it. Plus, you don't have major financial commitments to cover while you're "bootstrapping" and trying to get your new company off the ground. You look at what you might be giving up by giving entrepreneurialism a try and decide that your opportunity costs aren't very high. If your business doesn't make it, you can always go back to interviewing with larger companies while living with mom and dad. Your youth gives you the time to make up for mistakes, and that allows you to take risks that older people can't.

You're Never Too Young to be an Entrepreneur

You're Too Young To...	You're Young Enough That...
Know what you're doing	You have energy, optimism and drive
Be responsible	The world hasn't beaten the passion out of you
Be trusted	You can bounce back from losses and failures
Be careful	You don't know any better (you don't know "what
Know anyone (have contacts)	can't be done", so you just do it)
Have saved any money	You don't have to be "re-educated" or "re-trained"
Have any experience	You're impatient
Be taken seriously	You can change the world
Be accountable	

The next time someone tells you you're too young to do something related to business, look at the list above and remind yourself that the benefits of youth far outweigh its liabilities.

There are, however, some pitfalls that come with being young that you should be aware of. Let's take a look at some of those.

MYTH #5: Being young is a drawback.

REALITY: Being young can be an entrepreneur's greatest asset.

THE DRAWBACKS OF YOUTH

You're probably very familiar with many of the drawbacks of youth. You've had them pounded into you by older people again and again: you can't sign a legally binding contract until you're eighteen; you will probably find it impossible to get a bank loan without an adult cosigner; you probably don't have much of a credit history, so suppliers won't extend credit to you. Most adults in the business world will look at you as someone who's not serious, who lacks credibility, and who doesn't have the first clue about what they're doing. These things aren't major drawbacks; they're just inconveniences—obstacles that can be overcome in most cases. We'll look at how later in this book.

The real drawbacks of youth are actually the same as the great benefits of it. Let's consider how some of your greatest attributes and strengths can become your greatest challenges if you're not careful.

The Double-Edged Sword of Optimism

Optimism is a great characteristic of many young people. Most entrepreneurs have an abundance of optimism, but young people in particular seem to have vast reserves of it.

Optimism is a fuel. It can propel you through obstacles that would stop the average person. When the average person is slumped over with his head in his hands, wondering why he can't get anyone to see the genius of his product and write him a check, the optimist will think past the moment, envisioning the day when his product is in every home in America and he's become a rock star of the business world. That ability to think positively -- what less optimistic people might call "the ability to convincingly and repeatedly delude oneself into persevering against all odds" -- is perhaps the entrepreneur's greatest asset, though you'll never find it on a balance sheet (don't worry if you don't get that joke—you will after the section on Financials).

Optimism is a double-edged sword. Optimism can be fuel, but it can also act like blinders. Optimists have a knack for glossing over risks and making forecasts and plans that are wildly unrealistic.

Optimism -- left unchecked -- can make a young person trying to speak seriously about a business with an adult sound foolish. If you make statements like "there are six billion people on Earth; I expect to sell my product to only 10 percent of them, meaning that I'll sell 600 million units," you will be treated as a child. (Making the "potential-market-is-so-large-that-I-only-need-a-small-percentage-of-it-to-succeed" argument is a very common mistake that entrepreneurs of all ages make.)

The best way to avoid the killing end of the optimism sword is this: Get into the habit of under-promising and over-delivering. Deliver more than you've promised, even if it means setting the bar for your business low at first.

Character-Based Weaknesses and Skill-Based Ones

The reason that others will judge you harshly if you're overly optimistic is because unchecked optimism can appear to be a character flaw. If there's something wrong with your character—you're careless or prone to not considering risks—it can be a very difficult thing to change. If your optimism continually gets the better of you, leading you to paint overly-rosy pictures of what you and your business can deliver, you risk losing credibility with people you need to have on your side. Don't let your optimism, a great strength for an entrepreneur, run rampant. Always be able to highlight risks to your scenarios and ideas, and explain how you intend to circumvent or overcome these challenges.

On the opposite end of the spectrum from character-based weaknesses are skill-based ones. Skill-based weaknesses are judged less harshly because they are easier to overcome. That is why if an interviewer ever asks you for a strength and weakness, give them a character-based strength and a skill-based weakness.

What does that mean? It means that the strengths you identify are things rooted in your character: honesty, dependability, loyalty, intelligence, creativity, and so on. On the other hand, when you discuss a weakness, make sure it's a skill-based one: you're not good at typing or have problems using spreadsheets, for example. Tell an interviewer a skill that you're weak at, and then explain what you're doing to address that weakness: "I know this position requires that I be proficient in Excel, and my weakness is that I don't have very much experience at using that kind of program. I've signed up for an online course in using Excel, though, and I'm a very fast learner."

Remember, the reason you highlight character-based strengths and skill-based weaknesses is that you can erase any skill-based weakness fairly easily; if you have a character-based weakness, that's a hard thing to fix.

Similarly, if you don't have a credit history, you can create one. If you can't get a loan from a bank, you can find other sources of capital. If you're not old enough to sign a contract, the worst that can happen is you have to wait a few years or find a cosigner. In comparison, if you have a character flaw—if you let your optimism impair your judgment and lead you to ignore risks and create unrealistic plans—that's a deep-rooted problem.

Here again, your youth can save you. You might have a character flaw, but at least you can stop reinforcing it and you have the rest of your life to fix it. Start by tempering your optimism by identifying all the risks you can, listing them, and explaining how you'll manage them. Later, in the financials section of this book, I'll show you other ways of dealing with compulsive optimism, such as making "bad case" scenarios and doing "sanity checks," among other things.

Action for Action's Sake

Impatience is another double-edged sword. Impatience can lead to action and an insistence on change. These can be good things, but you need to understand when the walls you're charging into are going to give way and when they're not. Energy, enthusiasm, and demand for change can remove many obstacles in a young entrepreneur's way, but some things require a more subtle approach. Sometimes, the world's not going to move at the pace you want it to, but you can't let that stop you.

For example, you may decide to start a babysitting business. Your business is going to offer tutoring to the kids you sit for, and you figure you can charge a lot more than other sitters do because of the teaching angle of your company. You plan your business, advertise, and expect to have fifty regular customers signed up within three months. After two months, though, you've only gotten ten customers, and you're getting frustrated.

You're way behind your forecasts and budget, you don't understand why more people aren't using your service, and you're wondering if the business idea really was all that great. The impatient, energetic part of you might think that you need to be more active—maybe print out another couple hundred fliers and go door-to-door passing them out, or spending more time trying to get more followers on social media.

If your original tactic of advertising with fliers hasn't worked, though, adding additional effort to it isn't likely to result in much more success. Action for action's sake alone is rarely a successful tactic.

Rather, suppress your impatience and energy and calmly analyze what could be going wrong. Are you targeting the right market with your ads? Is the "shotgun" approach of blanketing neighborhoods with fliers a good one, or should you use the "rifle"—a more directed approach of posting fliers at neighborhood shops where parents with younger kids go, or working with a local day-care center to promote your services to parents with young children? Are your prices too high? Are people satisfied with your service? After some quiet contemplation, you might decide to survey the customers you have to see what they like and don't like about what you offer. Based on the outcome of this, you may realize that you've been charging too much, and decide to cut your prices. You can also give a "referral incentive" to your customers—a coupon stating that for each new customer they refer to you, they'll receive two hours of free after-school babysitting/math tutoring for their child.

Drifting from the Target

Another negative of impatience is that it can take away your focus if the results you expected aren't materializing. You and your friends may start a business designing web sites for local restaurants. You figure you can sign a few customers pretty quickly and be making a couple thousand dollars a month by the end of your third month of operations.

Five months in, though, you find that a lot of restaurants just don't have the money to pay you to make a web site, or they think they can make their own. Your partners start drifting, spending less time on the business and more time playing basketball or hanging out with their other friends. Pretty soon, your interests start to drift, too, and the business goes into limbo.

There's a balance between being slow, cautious, and contemplative and being aggressive, fast, and action-oriented. The more you can maintain that balance, the greater your likelihood of success. Set realistic goals, and anticipate slow starts. Plan for the "bad case"; then, if something good does happen, it's more of a motivator. If your plan anticipated not three thousand a month in income within three months, but rather only five hundred in six months, then getting a two thousand dollar a month contract in Month Three isn't a failure, it's a reason to celebrate. Aiming low and beating expectations—at least when you're starting out—can be a better path than aiming really high and continually undershooting.

DEALING WITH NAYSAYERS

There will be people who will admire you because you're a young businessperson ("Look at all the young people out there wasting their lives; at least you're trying to realize your potential and do something new"). But there will also be people who won't take you seriously ("How can you seriously think of starting a company when you've never even worked for anyone before?").

If you encounter people who are reluctant to do business with you because they don't think you can handle the job, make them a no-risk proposition. You can offer a money-back guarantee. Or tell them that you'll do the job and they can pay you what they think it's worth afterward (including not paying you if they don't like the work you did). Give them references and try to convince them that you're different from other young people and that they can trust you to do a good job.

Because you're young, many people will be skeptical of your abilities; you need to work extra hard to prove them wrong. You need to hold yourself to a higher standard. If you do that, though—setting the bar higher than any competitor does—you'll eventually emerge as the highest quality provider of the service or product your business offers.

Before Starting on the Entrepreneurial Path

Potential entrepreneurs should ask themselves why they are taking the start-up path. Are you doing it for money? For freedom? Glamour? Are you going to be a part-time or a full-time entrepreneur? Do you have romanticized ideas of what being an entrepreneur means and are you prepared for the trade-offs, sacrifices, and possible setbacks?

If you have realistic expectations of yourself, your partners, and your business idea, it's far less likely you'll be disappointed with your results. A big reason many entrepreneurs give up on a business is that they are disappointed that their too-lofty expectations weren't met right away. Success takes time. The chance of you coming up with the Next Big Thing in American Business and striking it rich overnight is about the same as winning the lottery. Maybe less.

Know what you're getting yourself into, set realistic expectations, and be persistent. Of course, if you don't have a good business to begin with, all the character- and skill-based strengths in the world won't matter. Knowing if you've got an idea that could be a successful business is the topic of the next chapter.

The Five Myths of Entrepreneurialism

MYTH #1: You need money, special skills, or connections to be an entrepreneur.

REALITY: Anyone can be an entrepreneur; you don't need anything but the right frame of mind.

MYTH #2: Entrepreneurs are born with a gene that compels them to start businesses when they're young.

REALITY: Many entrepreneurs discover their calling only after years of going the corporate route.

MYTH #3: Owning a business is glamorous.

REALITY: Owning a business is hard work, with long hours, lots of stress, and a ton of struggle.

MYTH #4: Being successful means taking big risks.

REALITY: Success is about defense as well as offense; it's about minimizing risk, not just maximizing opportunity.

MYTH #5: Being young is a drawback.

REALITY: Being young can be an entrepreneur's greatest asset.

Part 2:

Thinking About the Business

## Chapter 4

What Kind of Business to Start

There are eight key steps you should take in deciding on a business to go into:

1. Identify a problem.

2. Ask yourself if a solution to the problem would be worthwhile.

3. Brainstorm for a solution.

4. Evaluate the possible solutions.

5. Do a "quick and dirty" analysis of the solution.

6. Use an analytic framework for a more thorough analysis.

7. Ask yourself other important questions about the business.

8. Evaluate the industry.

We'll go through each of these steps in detail here.

1. <u>Identify a Problem.</u>

Everyone's got an opinion. That's the great thing about America: we all have opinions, and we all think our opinions are worthwhile; we're not shy about sharing our views and ideas, either.

With opinions usually come gripes: people have complaints about something they own, think they know a better way for pizza to be delivered, moan about the lack of an iPhone app that can pay their parking meter, or complain about how difficult it is to find someone to take care of their pets when they're on vacation.

Where most people see problems, entrepreneurs see opportunities; whereas most people talk about their grievances, entrepreneurs act on these complaints, forming businesses that will make money by providing solutions to those problems.

Identifying a problem, then, is equivalent to identifying an opportunity. And since so many people have opinions and complaints about things, mining those complaints can point you in the direction of an interesting business solution.

2. <u>Ask Yourself if a Solution is Worthwhile.</u>

Finding a solution to a problem needs to be worthwhile on two levels: as the basis for a viable business and as something worth doing for you personally. Whether or not something is worthwhile to you personally is a very different question than whether or not it could be a successful product or business.

There are three things that should line up if you're going to be successful and wealthy in your line of work: 1) you should do something you love; 2) you should do something you're good at; and 3) there should be a market for what you're doing.

We'll evaluate Point Three later in this chapter. Evaluating the size and potential of a market isn't that difficult, and many people can analyze a particular market and come to a good conclusion about whether or not that market is big enough to accommodate a successful business. Points One and Two, though, are things that only you can decide upon, based on your own passions, talents and values.

Passion and Belief

Entrepreneurs are salespeople. They are people who have to demonstrate the value of their product or service, sometimes shamelessly pitching it to complete strangers or to people who will tell them time and again they have no interest in what's being sold. Entrepreneurs don't just have to sell a product, though; oftentimes they have to sell the idea of a business to a bank loan officer in order to get money to buy equipment, or sell the idea to suppliers of key products who might be reluctant to supply some new, unknown, and untested company.

The key attribute of a good salesperson is passion, and passion usually comes from belief. If you really believe in the product or service you're selling, your passion will shine through to everyone you meet. Passion is contagious. Remember Michael Scott from the TV show *The Office*? That guy, for all his flaws, loved the paper business and honestly believed he was doing something good for people by selling them Dunder Mifflin paper. If you were in charge of buying office supplies for your company and some dispassionate person from a large paper or office supply company came to see you, giving you a memorized and monotone pitch about why you should buy their paper, and then Michael Scott came in to do the same sales pitch with much more exuberance, energy, and enthusiasm, you'd probably buy from Dunder Mifflin.

If you don't feel passionate about something, you're probably not going to be a good representative of it. And if you don't really believe in something, you're probably not going to feel passionate about it. If you don't feel passionate about something, it's going to be very hard to motivate yourself to keep at it, whether it's making you a lot of money or not.

When you think about a potential business, ask yourself if you really believe in that business; if you can really be passionate about it. If you think there's a need for a better paper or office supply company, you could form one to address that need. But unless you feel the type of passion for your product that Michael Scott feels for his, it's going to be very difficult for you to compete with the Michaels of the world, despite how incompetent those people might be in so many other areas.

Aptitude and Critical Success Factors

Are you good at what you're thinking of getting into? If your business idea is providing math tutoring to young children in lieu of babysitting them, you really need to be good at two things: math, of course, but more importantly you need to be good at communicating with young kids. You might be a mathematical genius, but if you don't know how to talk to a young child, you're not likely to be a very successful math tutor. You'll also need to know how to communicate with the real customer –- the kid's parents -- since they're the ones who will be paying you and will want to make sure you can deliver what you claim you can.

Identify the key things you need to be good at in a particular business. In business terms, these are known as "success factors." Someone thinking of opening a restaurant might think that the key success factor is being a good cook. This is not always the case. What is the most successful restaurant in history? The answer – at least in terms of sales and profits – is McDonald's. Does McDonald's make the world's best hamburger? I don't think anyone, regardless of how much they love that company, would say they make the best hamburger on the planet. Why, then, are they so successful? Maybe because they've identified and mastered other success factors for restaurants that most other food-service companies do not look at or get right, like standardization, site selection, and value.

McDonald's knows that offering a consistent, standard, pretty-good meal at a reasonable price in a high-traffic location will generate more success (as measured in dollars) than running the world's best restaurant, but having only one location and serving only a handful of diners a day.

Because the food and service at McDonalds are consistent across the world, customers know what to expect when they go into one. This makes it harder for customers to be disappointed. If you were to go into a new restaurant and order a $25 burger, you might complain that the service wasn't good or that the place forgot the pickles; you're unlikely to do that with a place you're familiar with (your expectations are already formed, and McD's knows how to manage to those expectations), and you're less apt to complain about a relatively inexpensive product than one that sells for a higher price.

In other words, the critical success factor for McDonald's might be standardization rather than food quality.

Understand what the critical success factors are in the business solution you're considering. For McDonald's the critical factor isn't just making a great hamburger, but making a great hamburger millions of times a day, every day, no matter how busy they are, and having all the hamburgers taste the same (so that people don't get disappointed that the hamburger they're having today isn't as good as the one they ate yesterday). If you are aiming to compete with Mickey-D's, ask yourself if you're really good at all of the things they are, or just one of them (being a great cook or being able to make a great burger). Can you beat McDonald's at its own game, or do you need to take a completely different approach to making burgers?

If you've identified what it takes to succeed, are passionate about your business, and are good at delivering the critical success factors, then you're on your way to having a successful and rewarding business.

Let's suppose you've identified an opportunity -- a solution to a problem. The product you could deliver is something that you feel passionate about, and you're able to deliver the critical success factors. What other things should you consider?

Conscience

Ask yourself if the business you're thinking about is something you can feel good about. Is it something you can be proud of? Is it something that does good? Is it safe?

These might sound like "fluffy", sentimental questions, but they're important ones to ask. A great investor I know once walked away from buying a very profitable company because that company made handguns, and the investor couldn't stomach the idea of owning a business that made products that killed people.

A lot of people would argue with that decision: They might say that making good handguns helps protect our soldiers and police officers. But the investor was making a judgment based on his own values, and at the end of the day he's the one that has to go to sleep with his conscience.

You might be initially enthusiastic about a business that you know, deep down, isn't in line with your values. If that's the case, either your values will change or your conscience will get the better of you, and your passion for the business will turn to disdain.

Simplicity

Is the business simple? Simplicity is a great thing. Look at the beauty of the old Apple iPod, precursor to the iPhone.

When Sony, Samsung, and other companies were making fancier and more complicated products with lots of bells and whistles, Apple came along and delivered a simple-looking white rectangle that stored and played music. It wasn't trying to be a machine that controlled your television, started your car, and toasted your bagel; it was just a small music-playing device.

There's simplicity of design and simplicity of product. The iPod had both: It looked simple, and if someone asked you what it does, you wouldn't have to use a lot of fancy jargon or have an advanced engineering degree to explain it to them. You'd simply explain, "It stores and plays my music."

Simple businesses have a lot of advantages over complex ones.

One area of complexity is regulation. If you're thinking of starting a business in an industry in which there are a lot of regulations, or with a lot of different government agencies that you have to answer to, you're going to have a lot more frustration and lost focus than the person who starts a business that isn't regulated.

Complexity in process is another type of problem. If you have a product that requires fifteen different stages of manufacturing, then there's a much greater chance that something will go wrong than if you just bought a finished product and sold it in one simple step.

Complexity can come in forms that aren't easily visible at first. For example, suppose your idea for a business requires a big up-front investment and ongoing large infusions of capital to keep it going. We'll look at things like cost structures later in this book, but a capital-intensive business (one that requires a lot of money to start up and operate) is financially more complex than one that's not capital intensive, if for no other reason than the capital-intensive business relies on money always being available. That's a layer of uncertainty and complexity that a business that doesn't require a lot of money to set up and operate doesn't have to deal with.

Finally, there's technological simplicity. In general, the more high-tech something is, the more complex it will be. There's a problem, however, with fast-changing, high-tech, and complex businesses: the chance of being blindsided is greatly increased. For example, Warren Buffet, the greatest investor that's ever lived and one of the wealthiest businesspeople on earth, usually avoids investing in tech companies. Why? Because he says he doesn't understand them. Does that mean he's not very smart? No, Buffet likes companies like Coca-Cola and Wrigley's more than Google or Facebook partially because, in effect, he says that in twenty years people will probably still be drinking Coke and chewing gum the way they do today. But it's not clear that they'll still be using Google's services or Facebook's products in the same way -- or that those companies will even exist in the future.

In a fast-changing industry like technology, a new product can emerge that will make the existing product obsolete. The iPhone might make GPS makers extinct; similarly, a new product that comes out tomorrow might make the iPhone obsolete. It's unlikely, however, that some new product will come around that will displace Starbucks, Coke, Wrigley's, Frito-Lay, or Kentucky Fried Chicken.

3. <u>Brainstorm for a Solution</u>

Let's say you've gotten through Steps 1 and 2: you've identified a problem, and you believe that delivering a solution to the problem could create a good business opportunity.

Not every new solution can be the basis of a good company. How can you know in advance if the idea you have is a good one -- one that can become a successful business and that has a market?

In this section, we'll look at a number of methods for evaluating a potential new businesses, analyzing a company's chances of success, and identifying the critical variables that determine if a good idea equates to a good business.

Brainstorm

Brainstorming is simply unedited, undirected, and unscripted thinking. It's identifying some problem, and then allowing any thought about the solution to the problem to come up and be developed. It works best in small groups or teams, but can be done on one's own.

When brainstorming, any possible solution can be proposed, discussed, added upon, and mapped out. By not rejecting any idea out of hand, brainstorming allows for a large number of ideas -- some conventional, some crazy, and some just very creative -- to come out and be expanded upon. Here are the steps of brainstorming on a business:

- **Identify the Problem:**
  Example: There's no grocery store in this area that sells organic produce.

- **Gather a Brainstorming Group:**
  You might try to get a group of five or more people together to brainstorm on solutions to the problem. Typically, your brainstorming group could be you and a few friends, but if you can bring in some people who know about business in general (a parent or other relative or a local businessperson) and someone who knows about the specific kind of business you're thinking about (in this case, someone who knows something about selling food), that would make the group even better. Be careful not to let the adults take over the conversation or create an atmosphere in which the younger people feel too intimidated to speak openly – try to draw out ideas from everyone in the group.

- **Brainstorm around the solution:**
  You should write down the problem and then invite any possible solutions, writing all of them down. You're not evaluating any idea right now, and you're not discouraging any idea. If someone feels that their ideas are being "shot down", they'll clam up, and you might miss out on a great comment. Remember, the craziest ideas sometimes lead to the most creative solutions.

4. <u>Evaluate the possible solutions</u>

Discuss the solutions identified in the brainstorming session. Some ideas might be eliminated, and others expanded upon. Brainstorming isn't expected to give you all the answers all the time, but it's a useful tool for drawing out different possibilities to consider when thinking about a potential new business idea.

5. <u>Do a Quick and Dirty Evaluation of the Business Concept</u>

Once you've identified a problem and brainstormed on solutions, you might have an idea that you think is a good one. During your brainstorming session, you discussed setting up a roadside stand that would sell organic produce, opening a store that would sell organic foods, starting a mail-order or internet-based business that would sell organic food, and renting booths at local street fairs to sell organic food you'd buy from a farmer in your area.

You decide to evaluate the idea of selling organic food through the Internet. You think you could get a simple web site up that would allow people to place orders for food that you could deliver once a week, on Saturday afternoons. The farmer you'd buy from would drive a truckload of food to your place on Saturday morning, you and your friends would split up the delivery into individual bags and then deliver them to the people who had placed the orders.

You've identified a problem, brainstormed on a lot of possible solutions, and have narrowed the ideas down to one that you want to evaluate more thoroughly. What to do now?

Understanding Your Market

First, you need to understand what your market would be. Who would buy your produce? To answer that, you probably need to know how much the vegetables would sell for. If the price, with delivery, is about the same as the vegetables in the supermarket, then you might be able to sell your organic food to everyone who buys vegetables. You'd be selling not only produce, but convenience: for about the same price as it costs to buy veggies at the market, your customers can have fresh, local, organic produce brought to their homes.

If the price is substantially higher than the veggies at the market, though, then you are aiming for a more specialized market: people who value the convenience of delivery and are willing to pay a lot more for organic food.

Who would pay more for groceries in return for not having to drive to the store every week? Perhaps busy people, the elderly or disabled, and people who don't have cars or access to the store.

Of course, to know what the price will be, you'll need to run some numbers. We'll go through how to determine things like costs and prices in detail in the Financials section of this book, but for now let's assume that the farmer says that he can bring produce to your house every week for 30 percent less than the cost of produce at the local supermarket. He says he'll need a minimum order of $500 a week to make the trip worthwhile.

You estimate that it would take you and your business partners about three hours to separate all the produce into small orders, and another three hours to deliver all the food. You figure that you'll spend an additional five to six hours a week taking orders over the Internet, accounting for the money the business brings in, and doing other managerial tasks. If you pay yourself and your friends $10 an hour for a total of 12 hours of work each week, you estimate you can make $380 a month by charging the same price that the grocery store does for its produce. (This analysis is intentionally kept very simple: It ignores the cost of gas, insurance, and other things.)

A Simple Revenue & Cost Analysis

Expected Number of Customers ("# of units") each week		50
Expected Sales per Customer ("revenue per unit")	$	20
Total Expected Revenues per Week	**$**	**1,000**
Expected Cost of Vegetables ("COGS")	$	500
Expected Labor Costs	$	120
Number of people working		3
Number of hours/person		4
Wage per hour	$	10
Total Operating Costs	**$**	**620**
Total Expected Net Profit	**$**	**380**

You now have a decent idea about how your business will work, what the main cost items will be, what you'll be providing to customers (good food and convenience), and how much money you could make. By selling vegetables at the same price that produce sells for at the supermarket, you figure you could sell to everyone who shops for produce at the market.

Let's take things to the next level, by doing two relatively simple types of analyses of the business idea.

6. <u>Frameworks to Evaluate Your Business Idea</u>

An analytic framework is just a structure that you can follow to evaluate something in more detail.

There are many different analytic frameworks that are used to evaluate business ideas, but two that are easy to use, common in many types of businesses, and taught in most business schools are SWOT and Porter's Five Forces analyses.

SWOT Analysis

The acronym SWOT stands for "Strengths, Weaknesses, Opportunities, and Threats." This type of analysis was developed by Albert Humphrey at Stanford University in the late 1960s, and is a simple way of thinking about different categories of a business.

The SWOT analysis is pretty self-explanatory: list your prospective business's major strengths and weaknesses; what you think the largest opportunities your company will face are; and the biggest threats to your company's business model.

There's not a lot of analysis that accompanies a SWOT; it's simply a framework to help you think about your business. Of course, if you have an easy time coming up with weaknesses and threats and a hard time identifying strengths and opportunities, that in itself should tell you something.

Here's what a SWOT analysis of the organic food delivery business idea might look like:

A SWOT Analysis for an Organic Food Delivery Business

Strengths
- Sole provider of a product with good demand
- Ability to sort and deliver product cheaply
- Low overhead (no store, low fixed costs)
- Convenient (internet-based) ordering system
Weaknesses
- Don't have a large advertising budget
- People don't know who we are; don't know if they can trust us
- Our product line is limited to vegetables
Opportunities
- Could expand product line (dairy, breads, meats)
- Could expand customer base (deliver to restaurants, senior centers)
- Potential to expand reach by recruiting kids from neighborhood for delivery
Threats
- Supermarket could start offering low-priced organic produce
- Easy for other people/companies to enter our business
- Regulatory threat if our product isn't high-quality (makes people sick) or if established competitors complain about our operation

Porter's Five Forces Analysis

Porter's Five Forces is named after Michael Porter, a professor at Harvard Business School who created the concept in 1979. According to Porter's method of analysis, there are five "forces" acting on any business, and you should attempt to measure "who has the power" in each of these. The five forces are: Supplier Power, Buyer Power, Threat of Substitutes, Degree of Rivalry, and Barriers to Entry.

We won't go through all of these areas in detail, but here's a brief examination of the Five Forces for your organic produce company.

a. Supplier Power:

Supplier power is the power of suppliers to set prices. The other forces we'll look at influence it, but essentially it's the amount of power that suppliers of a product or service have over the buyers of those goods or services.

Your company will be the "supplier" of organic food, conveniently delivered. How much "power" do you have over the buyers of this service? Can you raise your prices regularly without losing business? Is your product so much better than the alternative (driving to the grocery store) that customers will pay more for it? The amount of supplier power you have will be dependent on many things, including the other forces we'll examine.

An example of someone with a high degree of supplier power is U2, the rock band. There is only one U2, and if you want to see them in concert, you have to pay the most that they and their promoters think people are willing and able to. U2's uniqueness gives them a lot of supplier power, but it's not infinite; they realize that if they price their services (the cost of seeing them) too high, people might decide to do something else (choose a substitute to seeing U2 in concert). By contrast, the band at the bar downtown singing U2 songs can't get away with charging much for you to see them, as there are hundreds of other bands around the country that are just as good as they are (in other words, they're more of a commodity than U2 is).

An example of a company with a high degree of supplier power is Microsoft; if you need MS Office, you pay what Microsoft sets the software program's price at.

In most cases, the more "commoditized" your service or product is, the less supplier power you have.

The product your business sells is fairly unique: Organic vegetables are certainly different from standard ones, and the delivery aspect makes the product even more special. If you were just another person at the local farmer's market, standing at a table selling carrots and cabbages, you'd be just another commodity; there would be many other people there that would be selling those things, and the most likely things that would set you apart from other sellers would be a good location or lower prices.

The less "commoditized" your product is, the less you have to worry about competing just on price. In other words, the more differentiated and unique you can make your product from competitors' the more supplier power you will have.

b. Buyer Power:

This is the opposite of supplier power: it's the power of the buyer of a good or service over the supplier of that product.

Suppose there's only one organic farmer within driving distance of your house. Since he's the only supplier, he could potentially wield a lot of power over your business. If he sees that your business is doing well, he could jack up his prices and you'd have no alternative but to continue buying from him. On the other hand, if there are many organic farmers in the area that are willing to sell and deliver to you, then the larger number of suppliers of a commoditized product (one organic potato isn't that different from another) would suggest that supplier power is low and, conversely, that buyer power might be high.

An example of a company that has a lot of buyer power is Wal-Mart. Wal-Mart is the largest brick & mortar retailer in the country. If your company makes a toy car and wants to sell it at Wal-Mart, they will drive a very hard bargain with you. Unless your toy is so unique and in-demand that Wal-Mart feels they "must have it," you will probably find yourself accepting the terms and price that Wal-Mart sets. They have the buyer power to create a kind of "If you want to sell your toy here, this is what we'll give you," take-it-or-leave-it situation.

c. Threat of Substitutes:

This is the ability of a user to substitute your product or service with another one. The higher the level and availability of substitutes to what you offer, the less power you're likely to have as a supplier of your product or service to the market.

Substitutes aren't simply "obvious" ones. A Honda Accord is an obvious substitute for a Toyota Camry, but anything that buyers might do or choose that gives them a similar result to owning a car is a substitute. For example, riding the bus or riding a bike could be substitutes for buying a Toyota. In the U2 example given earlier, if the price of the U2 concert ticket is $100, you might "substitute" going to the concert with downloading a bunch of the group's songs for $20, going to a different concert for $25, or going to dinner and a movie for $50. A substitute for hiring a babysitter isn't just hiring a different sitter, but staying at home, taking the kids with you when you go out, or leaving the kids home alone (assuming they're old enough to take care of themselves, of course).

What are the substitutes for your organic vegetable business's product? The obvious one is "non-organic" vegetables: a person might decide to buy a non-organic turnip rather than your organic one. Less obvious substitutes might be frozen vegetables, meats or grains (if the price of vegetables rises a lot, people might cut back on them and use more chicken, bread, or fruit instead of veggies), growing one's own food (starting a garden at home), or eating out.

d. Degree of Rivalry:

This is basically a way of asking, "How intense is the competition?"

Gas stations have a high degree of rivalry: They advertise their prices on big signs every day, are all over the place, sell a commoditized product, and have to do everything possible (e.g., offer car washes or run in-house convenience stores) to get you to choose their station over any of the others. There is intense competition in that sector, just as there is in the restaurant business, lawn care business, and many other areas.

For your business, the most obvious rival would be markets that sell vegetables and, in particular, organic vegetables. If there are many supermarkets in your area, we can assume that there's a high degree of rivalry. The businesses would all advertise heavily, offer specials that would lure people in to buy certain things (and pick up some vegetables while they're at the store), know what its competitors are charging, and be able to switch its prices quickly in response to you or anyone else offering similar produce at more competitive prices.

e. Barriers to Entry:

This is a way of thinking about how easy or difficult it is for other people or firms to enter your business area.

Barriers to entry come in many forms: costs (if it costs $1 billion to build a semiconductor plant, there won't be a lot of new companies entering that industry); intellectual property, or IP (if you have a patent on a new type of hairdryer, no one else can make that product without paying you for the rights, and if you copyrighted a software program, no one can legally use it without paying you); reputation (if the doctor across the street has a sterling reputation, it might be very difficult for any new clinic in the area to compete with him); expertise; licenses; brand; and the list goes on and on.

Are the barriers to entry for your organic product business high or low? Considering that there are no special licenses required to sell your product (and, to keep things simple, let's assume there aren't), no specialized expertise, no major start-up or operating costs, that you don't yet have a "brand" or reputation that will keep people coming to you even if the local supermarket starts selling organic vegetables, and that the "switching costs" are low (it doesn't cost a customer anything to stop buying from you and switch to a different vegetable supplier), it would appear that the barriers to entry for the business you're considering are very low. In other words, just about anyone can enter this business and compete with you, so the "entry barriers" are low.

Illustration of Porter's Five Forces

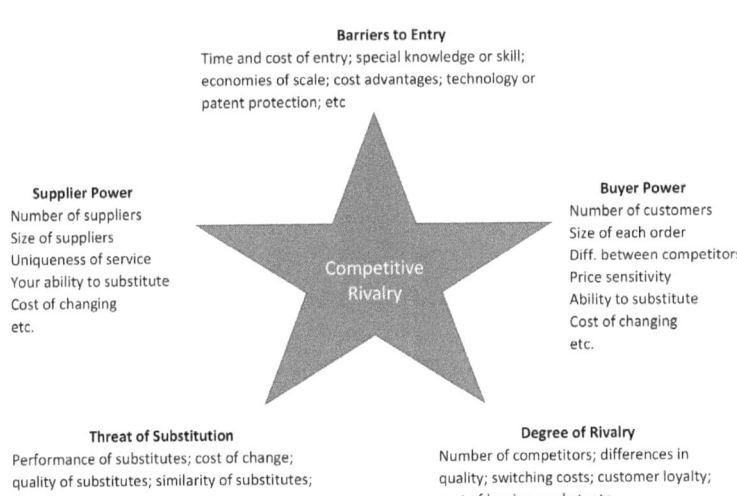

Barriers to Entry
Time and cost of entry; special knowledge or skill; economies of scale; cost advantages; technology or patent protection; etc

Supplier Power
Number of suppliers
Size of suppliers
Uniqueness of service
Your ability to substitute
Cost of changing
etc.

Competitive Rivalry

Buyer Power
Number of customers
Size of each order
Diff. between competitors
Price sensitivity
Ability to substitute
Cost of changing
etc.

Threat of Substitution
Performance of substitutes; cost of change; quality of substitutes; similarity of substitutes; ease of substitution; etc

Degree of Rivalry
Number of competitors; differences in quality; switching costs; customer loyalty; cost of leaving market; etc

SWOT and Porter's, Conclusion

Porter's and SWOT are by no means the only ways to think about and evaluate your business idea, but they're good places to start. They're easy to remember and apply, and they force you to consider many of the elements of your business that you might otherwise gloss over or forget to include.

Now that we've gone through the very casual (brainstorming) and more formal (SWOT and Porter's) ways of thinking about your potential business, we should consider a number of other things that every new entrepreneur should ask themselves about the business they're thinking of starting.

7. <u>Other Important Questions About the Business</u>

What are you Providing?

This may sound like a stupid question, but it's important that you think beyond the specific product or service your business is offering and understand what need it fills. This will help you identify why people might want your product, and what potential substitutes they have for it.

Consider a company we're all familiar with: Starbucks. What does Starbucks provide? Most people would say "coffee", but if you really think about it, you'll see that they provide much more than that. Howard Schulz, Starbucks's former CEO, believes that his company provides a "third place": a place outside of the home or the office that is inviting, comfortable, dependable, and familiar. For many people, the cost of a coffee is the "rent" they pay to relax on Starbucks's real estate -- the cost of having chairs and tables for an hour to meet with friends or the cost of having a couch to relax on. Starbucks also provides routine, and routine is comfort: Stopping by Starbucks every morning on the way to work or school is part of a daily ritual for millions of people -- as much a part of their morning routine as brushing their teeth.

When you think of it this way, the competition for Starbucks might not necessarily be Tully's or McDonald's, but a park, community center, or any other place that people might choose to meet at instead of Starbucks.

The organic vegetable business we looked at earlier is actually providing many things to its customers. It's providing vegetables, certainly, but it's also providing convenience (delivery), health, and peace of mind (many people will buy because they believe that organic foods are healthier or less harmful to the environment than non-organic foods are, and they feel good buying locally-sourced produce).

AN ASIDE: IS THE CUSTOMER ALWAYS RIGHT?

The idea that the customer is always right is a mistaken one. In blind taste tests, Pepsi scores higher than Coke does, a fact that led Coke to change its formula and offer "New Coke" many years ago—a decision that's viewed as one of the greatest business mistakes of all time.

You can see why Coke executives would have been worried: "People are telling us they like Pepsi more than Coke! We have to change the taste!" The problem was that people weren't actually saying that: people vote with their pocketbooks, and Coke consistently outsells Pepsi. The fact is that people are married to the Coke brand. Even if a competing product tastes better, people won't switch from the brand they love. Besides, how many people drink soda blindfolded anyway?

You could argue that the customer was right in this case—they did like the taste of Pepsi more—and that it was the company that was wrong in thinking that just because the customer liked the taste of Pepsi more they would switch brands. So, technically, the customer was right.)

Customers aren't very good at being right about things they want that are big departures from what's already available. What does this mean? Look at the Apple iPod as an example.

Before the iPod came out, most people were listening to music on portable CD or tape players.

Sony may have asked a number of customers what they wanted in a portable music player, and the customer, not being able to envision something radically different from the CD player they were used to carrying around, may have said "a smaller CD player" or "a CD that holds a lot more music." Sony went that route, promoting "evolutionary" products like "mini discs" and others that have faded into obscurity.

Apple, on the other hand, created something entirely different: they didn't look at the market as simply "CD players", but as "music delivery". Rather than create a product similar to a Sony CD player, they developed the iPod. The rest is history.

For revolutionary -- as opposed to evolutionary -- changes, customers often have no idea what they want. If you ask someone who travels a lot what they want, they might tell you something that's just a minor evolution of an existing product or service: "I want bigger seats in the airplane and shorter lines at the airport." You're not likely to hear someone say something revolutionary like, "I want to be able to teleport, making airlines and airports obsolete." That's an extreme example, of course, but you can get a sense of why the customer is usually more "right" when they're thinking of incremental change to existing products, or when, in the case of New Coke, factors such as "brand" and "loyalty" weren't factored in.

Is there a market for the product?

It's a common mistake to assume that just because you think something is a good idea that others will buy into it also. The best way to answer the question of whether or not there's a market for your product is to do some basic market research.

You don't have to be an expert in marketing to do good basic market research. For your vegetable business you could call a few supermarkets that sell organic produce and ask them if there's demand for the product (or visit the store and see if shoppers are considering the organic options they have there); you could contact your local markets and ask why they don't carry more organic foods (maybe they used to, but there was no demand for the product); or you could do surveys (ask 100 shoppers if they have ever bought organic, why or why not, and if they would consider buying organic if the price were roughly the same as non-organic and the food were delivered to them).

Here are some questions and suggestions for starting your market research:

a. Identify a company that is likely to be your competitor. Research the company and the product it has that yours would compete with. Make a list of the strengths and weaknesses of that company and its product, and a similar list of your company and product (even if your company and product are still just in your head right now).

b. Identify your potential market: Who buys the product your competitor produces? Why? What type of person is most likely to buy the competitor's product, and what type is most likely to buy yours?

c. Find some users of the competitor's product and find
    out what they like and don't like about the product.
    Would they recommend the product to a friend? Why
    or why not? It's very hard to take a customer away from
    a company they're satisfied with: would your success
    depend on taking away a competitors' customers, or
    would you be appealing to a group of users that your
    competitor hasn't addressed?

d. Have other companies tried to compete with the leader
    in the field and failed? Why? How could you be success-
    ful when they weren't?

e. How big is the market for your product, and what are the
    trends of the market? For example, the market for food
    catering might be over $100 billion nationally, but only
    about $250,000 in your town. The trend might be a decline
    in ethnic foods, to a rise in healthy, locally-grown options.

What's your competitive advantage?

This is an extremely important question. If you can't answer
it, you may want to rethink the business you're in.

A business's competitive advantage is the reason that
they're able to succeed when others fail; why people will want
to use their product or service rather than a competitor's.

There are many, many possible sources of competitive advantage: a business can be the cheapest provider of
something; offer the highest-quality product; have the fast-
est service; be in the most-convenient location; own the most
trustworthy brand; or have the smallest product or the largest. The competitive advantage also might not rely on the
product or service the business offers -- it could come from
being the first to market, having the best management or the
most money, or any number of other things.

Competitive advantages don't even have to be real -- they can simply be perceived: A successful lawn care business might not be the best or cheapest, but if people in the neighborhood see their friends using the company, they might assume that it's the best option and sign on as customers.

I bought a new laptop from an American PC maker and had some problems with the disk drive. After many calls to that company's customer service desk, I threw up my hands in frustration. I decided then and there that I would never buy another product from that company. The competitive advantage another PC maker might have over this company might not be a better PC, but a great customer service team. (If you're researching competitors, here's a simple test to put them through: Call their customer service number and count the number of buttons and the amount of time it takes you to get a real human being on the phone. A company that has a real person answering its phone and trying to help you with a problem scores much higher in my book than one that makes you navigate a maze of inputting numbers off the directions of a recorded voice.)

Whatever business you're in or thinking of getting into, you should be able to identify and easily explain what your competitive advantages are or will be.

What price should you charge?

There are a lot of ways to approach this question: you could set your prices based on what a competitor is charging (i.e. if you run a gym, you might charge slightly less than the gym down the road, or you might believe you can charge more because you offer things that they don't); you could make your financial models and set your prices at a level that will give you the profit you need to stay in business; or you can do market research to estimate how much your market would be willing to pay for what you're going to sell.

Another approach to consider in setting a sales price is asking yourself, "How much can I expect to sell and how much will it cost to produce and deliver my product or service?" Then, set a price that's some percentage over your cost. If that price is reasonable, you're on your way; if this "cost plus" (cost plus a profit) leads to a very high price, you need to go back to the drawing board and look at ways to lower your costs or accept a smaller profit.

Whatever you decide to base your price on, you will need to be able to explain and justify it to customers, lenders, investors, and others: "Why does your ice cream cost so much more than the one at the store down the street?" If you can't answer that question succinctly and persuasively, you could be in trouble.

The more data you've collected and analyzed and the more evidence you have that supports your price, the more persuasive the argument will be that people are willing to pay what you're asking.

Later in this book – in the Financials section -- we'll go through how to examine costs and volumes, something that will help you better analyze key factors to your business.

Is the business scalable?

This isn't an important topic if you don't ever expect to grow beyond a certain, smaller size, but it becomes relevant if you have ambitions to expand and become a large company one day.

Scalability is the ability of a company to grow efficiently. Some businesses are very scalable, and others aren't. An example of a highly-scalable business is Microsoft, which creates computer operating systems, puts those systems on discs, and then sells the software either online as a downloadable product, or (in some cases) physically, through the mail or at stores.

Microsoft can produce one million units of its product almost as easily as it can produce 100. Making an additional unit, or an additional million, just requires having more blank discs, downloading the original file more times, and putting more products in the mail (though these days most of their sales are from downloads over the internet). Furthermore, the company could do all of this from Bangalore, India, about as easily as it can from Boise, Idaho.

What's an example of a business that isn't very scalable? Something that depends on the talents of an individual, whose skills and abilities can't be duplicated easily. The world's best barber, for instance, can only cut so much hair. If he can't train other people to be fantastic barbers, then the amount of money he can make in his business is limited to how many people walk into his shop each day. Furthermore, if he's sick or on vacation, the business shuts down, and he can never expand by opening a second, third, or fourth shop.

A lawn mowing company might be fine to start up as an alternative to getting a summer job at Burger King, but it's probably not going to ever scale up and become a multimillion-dollar corporation. A lot of internet-based businesses, by contrast, are very scalable, as their owners don't have to do a much additional work to accommodate more viewers or users.

Is the business sustainable? Are there good long-term prospects for the business?

We looked at how high-tech products carry a risk of being blindsided and rendered obsolete through the emergence of new technology, but even some simple businesses can burn brightly, briefly, but turn to ash.

Pet rocks are the poster child of a fad that ended quickly, but every year there's a list of must-have Christmas toys that are garage sale pariahs by springtime. On the other hand, there are also toys that have become "sustainable," even iconic: Hot Wheels, Elmo, Thomas the Tank Engine, and Barbie, among others. Is your idea for a new sushi restaurant something that is likely to survive if a fad for Japanese food dies down?

Sustainability isn't determined just by the "trendiness" of a product, though. Increasingly, the term is used to describe environmentally-friendly products. A product that can be recycled is more sustainable than one that is used and thrown away. Similarly, sustainability can be based on economics: if the solar industry can't survive without massive government subsidies, then is it really a sustainable one?

What are the major risks?

An entrepreneur isn't someone who just takes advantage of opportunities; it's a person that is aware of the risks his business faces before, during, and after launch. In fact, more time should be spent working on minimizing risks than on maximizing opportunities: good things can take care of themselves; it's the bad things that will suck the time and energy away from you if you don't plan adequately.

Many people focus so much on the upside potential of their business idea, getting so carried away with the dream of success that they fail to consider the downside risks. When you actually launch your business, it's possible you'll be so busy "putting out small fires" (paying bills, collecting money owed from customers, dealing with employees or suppliers, handling insurance or regulatory issues, and doing the other small but necessary tasks to stay alive) that you won't be able to calmly evaluate business risks and how to minimize them.

It's not a lot of fun to think of all the things that could happen that could hurt or even kill your business, but isn't it much better to do this exercise before you launch a business than to find out afterward that something has gone wrong and you could lose everything (in some cases not just your business, but your personal assets, your credit, your parents' credit, your reputation, and more) because you failed to plan?

Brainstorm about every possible problem that could arise. Identify the ones that carry the greatest risk (that have either the greatest chance of occurring or that would do the most harm if they did occur) and try to find ways to minimize or eliminate those risks.

For example, with your organic vegetable business, what would happen if your farmer and sole supplier shut down the farm (lost it to the bank, retired, sold it, or just decided to stop growing organic food)? What would happen if someone got very ill from eating some of the food you provided and sued you and your company? What if the large grocery store down the street started offering cheap organic food? What happens if one of your delivery drivers hits someone while making a delivery? Or if someone finds out that the food you're selling as organic really isn't (maybe the farmer was mixing in regular produce with his organic product)?

Who could you find that is an expert on business and on business risk? Who can offer you some guidance, advice, and protection from your risks? The person or company that you or your parents buy insurance from would be a good place to start: Insurance professionals are in the business of assessing risk and "pricing it out." They can offer you insurance to protect you from many types of negative events. Maybe you should set up a meeting with an insurance agent and get their opinion of your business risks and ways to lower them. There might even be some insurance you could buy that would protect you from certain liabilities.

Lawyers and tax consultants can help, but they usually charge a lot for their services. You might be able to find and download useful contracts to use with suppliers (e.g. "if you fail to deliver your produce on time, you'll pay a penalty of $X" or "you promise that all the foods supplied will be certified organic unless otherwise stated"). It's not a great idea to skimp on legal and tax services, but if you shop around you can usually find good deals or at least cheap temporary solutions that will tide you over.

The type of business structure you choose will also give you some protection. We'll look at that, and also approaches to professional service providers, later in this book.

If you don't understand the risks of your business, you don't really understand the business. If you don't create strategies and use tools to minimize risk, all your "opportunity planning" could get washed down the drain.

8. <u>Evaluating Your Industry</u>

It's not enough to evaluate your own company; you must evaluate the industry the company will operate in. The Porter's Five Forces analysis is a great way to start the examination of your industry. Let's build on that analysis by looking at a few important questions you should ask and answer about the industry you're considering becoming a part of.

The Value of Luck and Timing

Never discount the value of good luck. A large number of successful people got where they are more from luck than from hard work, intelligence, or commitment. During the Internet bubble that burst in 2000–2001, you could have been a student with no business experience whatsoever, written a business plan in Crayola on a piece of toilet paper, and found people to give you millions of dollars to launch any business that had a ".com" in its name. Successfully launching the business had much more to do with the timing and type of business than it did on the abilities of management, the quality of the product, or any other factor.

Conversely, if you're trying to come to market with a new GPS device for automobiles, you're fighting an uphill battle:

smart phones have made stand-alone GPS devices all but obsolete. You could have the best dashboard-mounted GPS system ever seen, but you'd be fighting for a piece of a vanishing pie. As one of my business school professors used to say, "I have no doubt that the last buggy whip manufacturer in America made the country's best buggy whip," but when the horse and buggy industry was destroyed by the automobile, even the best buggy whip makers went under.

Luck is one of the most important factors for success in many endeavors, yet it gets the least amount of respect. Do you think Mark Zuckerberg or Elon Musk would have been as successful as they were if they had been born in North Korea? Probably not; these entrepreneurs were lucky to be born in the U.S. at a time of great technological change. You might get lucky and bring a product to market at just the right time; more often, though, you'll need to rely on your wits and hard work to get you to the top.

Many years ago, Burger King touted its "flame broiled" process of making hamburgers, which it believed created a burger that was much better than McDonald's traditional, grilled product. There was a major change in the industry, though, when customers started buying breakfast at hamburger chains: McDonald's was able to make eggs, sausages, pancakes, and other food on the same grills it used to cook hamburgers, while Burger King had to totally revamp its kitchens, spending a ton of money on new equipment, employee training, and additional space (you can't flame broil eggs and pancakes, after all). The "fast food breakfast rush" was a monumental change that was simply a lucky break for McDonald's and an unlucky one for Burger King.

Sometimes, your business gets a lucky break that propels it to success. It's just as possible, though, for the luck to fall your competitor's way, leaving you out in the cold. You can't plan for luck, but to paraphrase Samuel Goldwyn, "The harder you work, the luckier you'll get."

Industry Size and Growth

No business exists in a vacuum. Every company has suppliers, customers, competitors, and dynamics that need to be analyzed in the context of the industry it's in. Failing to understand the industry your company's a part of is a good way to end up in the trash bins of business history.

You've already looked at one method of analyzing your company vis-à-vis the industry it's in: Porter's Five Forces Analysis. In this section, we'll look at some things you would like to see in an industry that will put the wind in your business's sails rather than its bow.

Industry Characteristics that Can Be Good for Your Company

One venture capitalist puts it this way: "There are only three things I want to know: 1) Is the industry large? 2) Is the industry growing? And, 3) What share of the industry can your company get?"

If you're launching a business in a large and fast-growing industry, you'll have a much greater chance of success than if you launch in a small and shrinking one. The players in a dying industry fight fiercely for the last remaining scraps of business; you don't want to get caught in the middle of a price war with companies that have a lot more money than you do and could act irrationally.

It's much easier to be successful in a hot industry than a cold one. Compare Netflix and Redbox and the hot industry of non-traditional DVD distribution to once-hot-but-now-bankrupt DVD deliverers Blockbuster or Hollywood Video. Amazon or Apple might be the companies that displace Netflix and Redbox, before they, in turn, get knocked out by the next generation of movie-delivery technology company.

Being in a large growth industry is great, but for it to translate into real success, you'll have to become a significant player.

The share of the market you own, unsurprisingly known as your "market share," is important, but so is your share of the market to the total industry.

For example, you might believe you could get sixty percent of the market for your product, but if the product is only two percent of the industry, that might not be as attractive as getting twenty percent of a product that makes up thirty percent of the industry.

Confused? Look at it this way: Say you want to be a music producer and you're going to find and produce hip-hop albums. Sounds good—hip-hop is a big and growing market; it's also a significant portion of the overall music industry. There are a lot of hip-hop producers out there, but you figure you have a great niche: you're going to focus on Christian hip-hop artists. This might not be a bad idea at all. Christian music has a strong following, and other products (books, movies, TV shows) aimed at that segment of the market have been successful. If you can make a case that the Christian hip-hop market is large, expanding, and that you can take a big share of the industry because there aren't a lot of producers focusing on this area, you could have a great business.

On the other hand, if you wanted to produce country-western/hip-hop crossover albums—hip-hop albums for country western fans—you might be able to take a huge share of that market, but it would be such a small segment of the hip-hop and music industries that it probably wouldn't result in much success.

Competition

Sometimes, you should worry more about the lack of competitors than by the presence of them. You might think it's great that no one else is offering organic produce in your town, that it means the field is clear for takeoff and that you'll be the only (or at least the first) supplier. But the absence of competitors could also mean that there's no market for what you're planning to offer.

Some basic market research should help clarify if there's a real opportunity that others simply haven't identified, or if there's a good reason for the absence of competition.

Find companies that sell something similar to what you intend to offer, and try to find out if they've ever considered selling the product or service your business will sell. If they have, what happened? If they haven't, why not?

For example, if you plan to sell home-delivered organic produce, find out if companies selling organic food in your area ever delivered their product but gave up on the business, or if companies that do grocery delivery have ever delivered organic produce. If not, why not? If so, why aren't they still in that business?

Management

Having a good management team is very important, but that in itself is usually not enough to overcome the challenges of being in a bad business. To quote Warren Buffett: "When a great manager meets a bad business, it's usually the reputation of the business that stays intact."

Only a few superstar managers—people like Steve Jobs—can turn the tide of a company that is in decline. For every Steve Jobs, though, there are millions of managers who thought their talents could overcome the decline in their company or industry, but were proven wrong. For example, Jerry Yang of Yahoo! thought that he could restore his company's position as the leader in search engines; this prompted him to reject a generous offer from Microsoft to buy the company, and, eventually, to being fired by his board of directors.

Even a poor manager can run a great business, but a great manager rarely succeeds with a poor company.

Chapter 5:

Common Mistakes

I'll conclude this section of the book by looking at some pit-falls that young people fall into when deciding on a business. Many of these mistakes and pitfalls are based on the myths of entrepreneurism, and try to set the record straight.

COMMON MISTAKES AND MISCONCEPTIONS OF YOUNG ENTREPRENEURS

1. Focusing solely on invention and ignoring innovation

2. Not asking yourself why your product or service doesn't already exist

3. Being too optimistic about your budget

4. Expecting other people to make the business a success

5. Focusing on too narrow a customer group

6. Getting into very labor- or capital-intensive businesses

7. Coming up with far-fetched businesses

---

1. Focusing solely on invention and ignoring innovation

Entrepreneurs and inventors are two very different groups of people, but many people tend to believe that if they don't

73

invent some new product or service, they can't be successful entrepreneurs. That's far from the truth.

Rollin King and Herb Kelleher didn't invent the airplane or any part that goes in it, but they did create one of the most efficient and profitable airlines in the world, Southwest. King and Kelleher's genius lay in changing the business model of airlines, streamlining costs, and focusing on the customer (that may not sound revolutionary, but many of the "big name" American airlines treat their customers almost as annoyances, rather than as luxuries that need to be well-cared for).

Similarly, Michael Dell didn't invent the personal computer, but he created an approach to building and selling PCs that customers loved, and Dell has built the company into one of the most successful PC makers on Earth.

Craig Newmark didn't really invent anything when he started Craigslist, but he changed the way that classified ads -- once the domain of print newspapers -- could be posted and viewed.

The message should be obvious: You don't have to invent something new to make a great business. Identifying and filling an existing need can lead to great success.

A related myth is that your product has to be a fantastic, revolutionary one in order for the business to be successful. You don't have to start with a grandiose idea. Rather than launching a business that will try to take on Amazon or Facebook, why not start with one that tries to be the best in a narrower field, or launching in an area that isn't served by someone else (what Craigslist, LinkedIn, and Wikipedia all did)?

2. Not asking why your product or service doesn't already exist

In a class I taught on entrepreneurism for teenagers, one group of high school students came up with the idea of combining Wite-Out correction fluid with pens -- there would be a fixture at the top of the pen that would allow the user to Wite-Out any mistakes.

I could see the need for something like this, but there was one thing I couldn't understand: Bic, the giant company that makes, among other things, pens, owns the Wite-Out brand of correction fluid. If there were a need for a pen with a Wite-Out dispenser on it, why wasn't Bic making one?

There was another thing about the business idea that didn't make sense to me. A business like this could only have two outcomes: 1) the product was a flop, and the business would be shut down; 2) the product was a success, and Bic and other larger companies would create something very similar to take the market away. Even if you patented the product, you'd be paying Bic for the use of the Wite-Out, so how could you possibly hope to be cost competitive? (A key supplier for your product would be a competitor—why would they supply you at all?)

Some good ideas are truly unique. Others might not be unique, but you can make them a success by getting them to market quickly, offering great service, or otherwise differentiating your product from others out there. Some good ideas have been tried and tested, though, and are still found to fail.

A little market research—doing some homework on Bic would help make the case for or against a product like this. For example, finding out if Bic had ever tried a Wite-Out pen before or why a similar product (pens with erasers on them) was never very successful would be a very useful starting point.

3. Being too optimistic about your budget

A budget is composed of inflows (revenue from sales) and outflows (money spent on setting up and running the business). Most young entrepreneurs make two budget mistakes, the effects of which compound and create real problems for the company. First, they overestimate their revenues (remember earlier, when we talked about tempering your optimism and setting targets that were easy to hit or surpass at first?). Second, they underestimate their costs.

My advice in regard to estimating costs is the mirror image of the advice regarding revenues: make low estimates about how much money your firm will take in, and high estimates about how much you'll spend. In essence, you'll be making a worst-case scenario for your business. If you can stand the results of that scenario—that is, if you and your business can endure under those bad circumstances—then you're in a good position; chances are, your company will do better than your worst-case scenario assumes.

Overestimate your costs and underestimate your revenues. You'll be doing the opposite of what most young entrepreneurs do, and saving yourself a lot of heartache and stress by doing so.

One final thing: go out and investigate what real costs are. If you want to rent an office, don't assume you can get one for five hundred dollars just because that seems like a reasonable price to pay; go and find out exactly what an office would cost (rent, deposit, improvements, and other costs). Do the same for all your other major cost items.

4. Expecting other people to make the business a success

In my experience, there are two types of young entrepreneurs: those that intend to build the business themselves (or with people they have on board already) and those that expect to bring others into the business in the future. The problem with this second group of young would-be entrepreneurs is that they tend to overestimate their own importance and the ease with which they can recruit others.

I've dealt with a number of young people with business ideas in which the critical success factor is in the hands of someone else, usually some professional engineer that they hope to find, somewhere and somehow, without thinking of things from that person's view. For example, the following interaction is more common than you might think:

Young entrepreneur: My idea is to make a chip that you can put on children that will allow you to track them with your cell phone, so if a child is abducted, it would be easy for someone to find them.

Me: That sounds like a great idea for a product. What experience do you have with chips like this?

Young entrepreneur: Well, I don't have any, but I'll hire someone that will make the chip.

Me: Okay. Let's assume that there is someone out there who can do that. Why wouldn't she do it on her own, or with someone else? Why would a person like that—probably a very high-paid and senior engineer—decide to create a chip for a sixteen-year-old's company?

Young entrepreneur: Because I had the idea.

If you don't have the resources to build the business yourself, or have a team that is already committed to the company, don't assume you're going to find someone that's going to: a) be able to do what you need them to; and b) be willing to work for a person much younger and less experienced than they are.

Ideas are cheap. Create a business, make some cash, build a reputation, learn and grow, and raise some real money. You'll then be in a position to approach a star engineer at Google or Intel and perhaps get them to jump ship and join you on your quest.

5. *Focusing on too narrow a customer group*

Your customers might not be the people you expect them to be, or even people at all. No, I'm not talking about businesses aimed at pets (thought that might be the best market for your company) – your target market might be other companies, government organizations, non-profit organizations or other countries.

In one of my classes many years ago, an entrepreneur came in and demonstrated an LED light bulb when those things were still new and novel. The bulb looked like any other, but could put off 100 watts without getting hot and while consuming a small fraction of the electricity that an incandescent bulb does (meaning it would have to be changed only once every ten years or so). The problem: the bulb would cost a consumer about $35 (remember, this was a long time ago, when prices were still very high), versus only about $2 for a traditional bulb. Even if the consumer knew that the bulb was more environmentally friendly than a regular bulb and would save them $5–6 per year in electricity costs, most people simply will not pay $35 for a light bulb.

So maybe the market shouldn't be people.

Who would be willing to pay $35 or more for a light bulb? What about companies or organizations that have to spend much more than that changing bulbs? And who would that be?

Suppose those bulbs were used to illuminate stoplights at busy intersections. With an incandescent bulb that burns out frequently, the city might have to send a crew to the intersection, stop traffic for hours, use specialized equipment to lift someone up to change the bulb, and then run tests to ensure that the light is working. A simple changing of a burned-out light bulb could cost the city thousands of dollars.

The customer, then, wouldn't be a person, but a government organization. That organization might be willing to pay a thousand dollars or more for the LED bulb, knowing that even at that price they'd still save a bundle on bulb replacement.

Or maybe the customer would be a branch of the military, or an airline, or a nonprofit organization that needs highly energy efficient lights for schools they're building in a developing country, where finding replacement bulbs could be a real challenge.

Suppose you're thinking of starting a company that will dig-itize old books. Rather than focusing on individual consumers, you could approach your local library or school system – one order from a library could be worth more than 500 orders from individuals. If your business is babysitting, maybe you could approach your PTA about sitting for a number of kids during their next meeting, allowing parents to attend while their kids are looked after in the school's gym. If your company sells sun-glasses, perhaps you should try selling to a local skateboard-ing shop or sporting goods store, a place that would buy your glasses by the case, rather than to kids at school, who'll buy only one pair at a time.

Don't assume that the best customer for your product is a person like you; it might be someone, or something, very dif-ferent.

6. Getting into very labor- or capital-intensive businesses

Remember the discussion about being able to "scale up" a business? Businesses that are labor- or capital-intensive -- that require a lot of labor or money to produce a product or service -- are difficult and costly to scale up to a large company.

In our example of the barbershop from the section on scal-ability, we see a business that is very labor-intensive: One barber might be able to do 10 haircuts a day, charging $15 for each and making a profit (after rent, insurance, and other items) of ten dollars per cut, or $100 per day. If that barber worked 300 days a year, he or she would make $30,000—not very much for someone working so hard.

Babysitting is another example of a labor-intensive busi-ness. If you're thinking of starting a babysitting business with a friend, then your sales and profits are limited by how many hours you're able to work each week. If you want to grow the business, it means hiring someone else. Keep in mind that bringing on an employee means doing payroll, adding a lot of tax work, paying social security and taking on other costs for the worker, as well as a host of other tasks for yourself. Scaling up by adding people isn't a very efficient way to grow your business.

Many young people tend to "think small" about their abilities to offer services. People with babysitting experience, for example, try to set up a business in which they babysit; people with experience mowing lawns set up lawn mowing businesses.

See if you can use your experience not to do the work itself, but to hire and train others to do the work for you. Instead of mowing lawns yourself, you could create a company that finds students who want to earn money doing yard work, train them, give them uniforms (a great way to make them look professional and "brand" your company), and dispatch them to the homes of customers you find. If you were to do this, you could scale your business easily, sending teams of kids out to do the actual yard work for $12 an hour, while you get 25 percent of that—three dollars an hour—for finding the customer, guaranteeing the quality of the work, and providing equipment, training, and maybe insurance. Three dollars an hour doesn't sound like much, but if you got to a point where you were managing twenty teams of people working three hours a day, you'd be making $180 a day for your managerial efforts.

Use your mind rather than your muscle or time. Be a manager rather than an employee or laborer. Set up a business that can grow to ten times its initial size without requiring ten times the capital or labor.

7. Coming up with Far-Fetched Businesses

A final mistake young people make is coming up with far-fetched business ideas. I've seen 16-year-olds come up with business ideas that would take years to launch, large teams of people to manage, and millions of dollars in spending, all for products or services that might be so unrealistic that they simply can't be provided profitably.

"I am going to create a small battery pack that can fit into the trunk of any older car and allow the driver to switch between driving with gas and driving with the battery." That sounds like a great idea, but the reality is that it could possibly be an overwhelming challenge for a young person with limited capital, time, and other resources. What about scaling down the business idea a bit to something like "I am going to create a simple measuring device that will allow drivers to see how much carbon dioxide their vehicles are emitting while they drive"? Creating a device that measures emissions seems to be a lot more "do-able" than making something that challenges the entire design and mechanics of vehicles in general.

Try to identify a business that you could set up and run in realistic time frames (i.e. set up within six months and run while working no more than twenty hours a week during the school year and forty hours a week during vacations) while requiring no more money than you have available right now or can get within a few weeks.

Part 3:

Planning Your Business

## Chapter 6

The Planning Process

If you've decided that you want to start your own business, then this section of the book will show you some of the "pre-launch" processes you should follow. The most important of these first steps to launching your business is making good plans.

Planning is the most important part of launching a business that people tend to neglect. Unfortunately, many entrepreneurs assume that since they've spent so much time thinking about their business idea they don't need to go through the "formal" work of making plans. Other entrepreneurs believe that their idea is so time-sensitive they "don't have time" to do the planning.

In this section, we'll look at why planning is so important, what types of plans should be made and how to make them, and cases in which planning might be minimized or even skipped.

WHAT IS PLANNING?

Planning is the formal process of identifying key areas of a business idea, anticipating how your business will address those areas, evaluating the positives and negatives of alternative approaches, and documenting the idea thoroughly so that it can serve as a blueprint for company management and a resource to other people involved with your business.

Good planning takes a lot of time and effort. It doesn't have to be hard—it doesn't usually involve any higher math, complex science, or particular expertise. But good plans are thorough, and that means time-consuming. The good news is that once your plan is made, it's easy to modify, and a good plan will pay for itself many, many times over.

Planning is not just thinking about a business. For an entrepreneur, thinking about your business is something that's almost impossible not to do: You'll think about it when you're sleeping, showering, eating, and exercising. Thinking is often an automatic process; planning is a deliberate one. You can't plan without thinking, but making plans is a big leap from simply thinking about something.

Planning is an important part of any kind of strategic endeavor: combat, sports, chess, business, and anything else that requires strategy. There's never been a winning football coach that sent his team out on the field without a plan, trusting that the team's natural talent and abilities alone would win the game. Business is more difficult than any sport; if you think you can throw your team — your product, your management, and the other things associated with your company — onto the field without a plan and come out ahead, you'll probably end up with a losing record.

Planning has to take place before the business launch. If you're looking at starting a real, full-time business that can earn you enough money to live on (not just while in school, but well afterward) then you'll probably be so busy after launching that you won't have time to catch your breath, much less do any serious strategic thinking. Start the planning process months before your business launch.

You'll find that the planning process will teach you and others associated with the business a lot about what needs to be focused on. You'll also find that good planning can prevent many dangerous problems. In most areas, it's a lot harder to fix a problem after the fact than to prevent one from occurring; if you don't plan, you could end up with a company that has problems that cannot be repaired. You would probably have to shut the business down and start all over again, knowing that you will need to plan for the second go-around. Don't go through all the effort of starting a business without making a plan.

THE IMPORTANCE OF PLANNING

Many people, especially those who think their ideas are very time-sensitive (if they don't launch right away, their window of opportunity will shut), are so eager to start operating that they skip the planning stage, thinking, *"Who has time to make a bunch of financial models and write a detailed business plan, when I could be making money every day?"* If you've gotten this far, you've probably already given a lot of thought to your business idea, and you might feel that's enough -- that you've thought through everything and don't need to take the step of actually writing things out in detail.

You should understand that the time and effort you put into the planning process will be the most important investment you'll ever make in your business and the one that will give you the greatest return. Proper planning will allow you to put many of the abstract thoughts about the business into concrete form—hopefully a form that bank loan officers, investors, suppliers, customers, and partners can easily understand.

Good planning is the best and cheapest way to reduce your risk. You could find, through the planning process, that the idea of selling your product in retail outlets will end up losing money for your business, whereas selling through a wholesaler will make a good profit. Or you might learn that you could charge much more for your product or service than you had anticipated.

Similarly, planning could lead you to choose a business structure that protects your personal property and that of any co-signers you might have. A good operating agreement could nip any big disagreement with your partners in the bud. And you'd be surprised at how many companies think they're making money on each product they sell but, because they haven't done a break-even analysis, find later that each product sold was losing the firm money.

Thorough planning for your business takes time and effort. It can be the most painful part of the "company birthing process."

There will be parts of the planning process that you'll find difficult and frustrating and that will make you want to give up and jump ahead to launching the company quickly. For the vast majority of companies, though, this stage is what will separate the successes from the failures. Remember: Other people, many with less motivation and skill than you, have done this. You can do it, and the next few chapters will try to make it as painless as possible.

GETTING A FREE LUNCH

You've probably heard the expression, "There's no such thing as a free lunch." This means that there's a cost for everything.

The reality is that there are some free lunches. Good planning can create one for you. To explain this, we need to look at the relationship between risk and return.

Risk and return are related to one another. Usually, when risk is low, returns are low; when risk is high, returns are high. This is why the stock market, over the long-term, returns more than, say, a savings bond: the stock market is riskier than an investment in the U.S. government (which is what a savings bond is), so investors in the stock market demand a higher return for the additional risk they're taking with their money.

When someone tells you there's no such thing as a free lunch, they mean that you have to give up something to get something. In the investment world, that means that if you want to make more money, you have to take more risk.

Planning is the best way to get more return without taking more risk. You see, start-up businesses are risky (the Small Business Administration reports that half fail within their first 12 months), and this is part of their appeal: many people who start a company and many people who invest in them expect that while the chances of success might not be great, the payout for success could be huge.

The reason that planning is so important is that it usually lowers the risk of failure without lowering the return of the business. In other words, it's a free lunch (well, almost free—it does take some time). A business that has a 50 percent chance of failing might be able to lower that to 30 percent with a good plan; a business that might lose $100,000 before realizing things weren't fixable might be able to cut those losses substantially if it has a plan that identifies what could cause the bleeding and allows management to address problems early. A good plan reduces risk without reducing the potential upside of the business.

Planning is a way to help you leave nothing to chance. The more risk you can eliminate before you start your business, the greater the chance of its success.

TYPES OF PLANS AND THE PURPOSES OF EACH

There are different types of plans and different things to consider for each. The most common plan is known, not surprisingly, as the Business Plan. This is a document that most businesspeople are familiar with, and that most professionals will expect of you.

However, before you can create your business plan, you will first need to decide upon the structure of your business, as this will help set the stage for writing the business plan.

## Chapter 7

Choosing Your Business Structure

There are many different types of companies you can set up. Each company needs a business structure, though, and there are only a handful of structures to choose from. Each structure has its own positives and negatives. Choosing a business structure that fits your needs is the first step in planning for the business.

The main types of business structures are the following:
- Sole Proprietorship
- General Partnership
- Limited Liability Company
- Corporation

We'll look at each of these types of structures, examining the positives and negatives of each one.

CONSIDERATIONS FOR YOUR BUSINESS STRUCTURE

Generally speaking, there is a trade-off between the simplicity of creating a company and the protection it gives you. In other words, you could choose a corporate structure that is very easy to set up but that doesn't protect you well. You could also choose a more complex structure, but one that gives you better protection.

"Protection" for an entrepreneur comes in two key forms: protection from liability and protection from double taxation. Liability should be your first concern.

A liability is an obligation that legally binds you to another person or company to settle debts and fulfill other commitments. Owing money on a loan or on a lease are examples of liabilities. Some corporate structures can shield you from "unlimited liability", meaning that they can prevent other people from going after assets outside those of your company's.

For example, suppose you started a company that did hair and makeup work for teen girls. One day, an employee of yours turns the water on too hot for a shampoo, and burns the scalp of a customer. The customer files a lawsuit against your company, seeking $20,000 in damages. Your company has assets of only $5,000. If you had a corporate structure that limited your liability in this type of event, the customer would only be able to go after the $5,000 in net assets your business has; it would be unlikely that she could win a judgment giving her your personal (non-business) assets, such as your car, money in your savings account, and so on. If, however, your corporate structure did not protect you from personal liability, then that customer could also win a judgment giving her your personal assets.

Tax benefits are a little trickier, since tax laws change fairly often, but one general concept that you need to be familiar with and that hasn't changed in many years is the concept of "double taxation."

Double Taxation

Double taxation is just what its name implies: being taxed twice. Most people dislike paying taxes once; imagine having to pay them twice on your business. If a business pays a salary or wage to someone—including you, the owner—that payment is an expense to the business, and the company doesn't have to pay tax on that amount. If the business has profits after all of its expenses, then it can pay those profits out to owners as dividends, but those dividends are effectively taxed twice—at the business level and at the individual level.

Don't be alarmed if that sounds confusing to you. Let's look at this concept in more detail and see what it means and what the impact is.

Case 1:

In the following scenario (see the box below), John owns a business that makes $10,000 a month in revenues. He doesn't pay himself a salary (the "labor" expense is zero), but takes out all the profit ($2,100 after taxes) from the business at the end of each month.

The profit he takes from the company is classified by the IRS as a dividend, and John will pay taxes on the dividend income he receives. Taxes on dividends usually range from zero to fifteen percent, but we'll use fifteen percent in our example.

So, if John's company makes a profit of $2,100 in profit each month, and John takes all of that as a dividend he will pay $315 each month in taxes for that dividend income.

But John's company is paying taxes also: It's paying $900 each month in taxes on the $10,000 in sales it has. Thus, John is paying taxes twice: $900 on the company level, and $315 on the dividends he's received personally. His total taxes are $1,215 each month.

Paying Yourself as an Owner (more taxes)...

Case 1: No Salary, Take Out Profits	
Step 1: Business has $10,000 of revenues and pays nothing in salaries	
Total Revenues	**$ 10,000.00**
Costs:	
Materials	$ (5,000.00)
Labor	Zero
Other expenses	$ (2,000.00)
Total Expenses	$ (7,000.00)
Operating Profits	$ 3,000.00
Tax (30%)	$ (900.00)
Net Profit	**$ 2,100.00**
Step 2: Owner "takes out" the net profit in the form of dividends	
Dividend to owner	$ 2,100.00
Tax on dividend (15%)	$ (315.00)
Total after-tax income	**$ 1,785.00**
Step 3: Calculating taxes paid and income received	
Taxes paid by business on profits	$ 900.00
Taxes paid by owner on dividend income	$ 315.00
Total Taxes Paid	**$ 1,215.00**
Total after-tax income received by owner	**$ 1,785.00**

Case 2:

John sets his salary so that it "eats up" all the profit of the business. In other words, his salary will vary month to month, but will be set so that there is no profit left in the company, so there will be no dividends to be paid out.

In this case, there's no tax for the business, since the business is not showing any profits; John pays tax only on the salary he's received. If we assume that his income tax rate is 25 percent, then the total amount of tax he'll pay is $750—zero tax on the business-entity level and $750 on the income he received. His total after-tax income is therefore $2,250. Total taxes paid: $750.

...Compared to Paying Yourself as an Employee (less taxes)

Case 2: Owner takes a salary and no dividend		
Step 1: Business has $10,000 of revenues and pays $3,000 in salaries		
Total Revenues	$	10,000.00
Costs:		
Materials	$	(5,000.00)
Labor	$	(3,000.00)
Other expenses	$	(2,000.00)
Total Expenses	$	(10,000.00)
Operating Profits	$	-
Tax (30%)	$	-
Net Profit	$	-
Step 2: No profits left to pay out (as dividends); all income in the form of salary		
Dividend to owner	$	3,000.00
Tax on salary (25%)	$	(750.00)
Total after-tax income	$	2,250.00
Step 3: Calculating taxes paid and income received		
Taxes paid by business on profits	$	-
Taxes paid by owner on salary income	$	750.00
Total Taxes Paid	$	750.00
Total after-tax income received by owner	$	2,250.00

The above is an extreme example, used to illustrate the effects of double taxation. I'm not suggesting you try to manipulate your books so that your company never shows a profit (in fact, you're likely to get into trouble with the IRS if you do that); I'm just showing you that different business structures have different tax treatments.

The owner of a company can pay less in taxes and take home more income by being taxed once rather than twice. That statement shouldn't sound surprising, but the key is to have a business structure that allows any profits to be "passed through" to the owner, rather than taxed and then distributed as dividends. The ability to avoid double taxation is a key reason that most people choose to operate as an LLC or GP, rather than as a corporation.

Now, let's take this knowledge of the types of protection that you need to consider into the next section, choosing the best type of structure for your company.

IS IT WRONG TO AVOID TAXES?

"There are only two certainties in life: death and taxes." This well-known saying may be true, but it doesn't stop people from trying to cheat either death or the IRS. The thing is, you don't get anything from dying, but you get a lot of important things from paying taxes. Police forces, fire departments, the military, schools, the national park system, social security, and a host of other things are provided by the tax dollars that individuals and companies pay. Whether you use any of these things or not directly, we all share in the benefit of these services, and we all have an obligation to bear our share of the costs.

The government realizes, though, that small businesses are the lifeblood of the economy, and they encourage entrepreneurs to start companies and create jobs. One of the ways they do this is by offering businesses certain tax breaks. By helping companies keep their taxes down (by making things like salaries tax deductible), the government helps business owners keep "more money in their pockets," which could lead to the company hiring more people. The people the businesses hire pay taxes on the money they earn. In fact, our government ends up making more in taxes from the people that businesses hire and employ than it gives up in tax breaks to the businesses themselves.

It's important to understand that taxes help all of us. They help our country remain the land of opportunity that it is. Take advantage of the tax incentives the government gives to you as a small businessperson, but don't become preoccupied with not paying your fair share.

TYPES OF BUSINESS STRUCTURES

Sole Proprietorship

A Sole Proprietorship (SP) is the easiest type of company to set up. You don't need to register with your state, get an EIN (something we'll go through in detail later), or file a fictitious business name (also known as a "Doing Business As", or D.B.A.) application. Basically, you just start operating your business and file a form called a "Schedule C" on your taxes. It's as easy as that. Kim could decide today that she wants to start a babysitting business, and "Kim's Home Childcare" is born, just like that. Kim will need to separate her company income and expenses from any other income and expenses— something we'll discuss in more detail later—and she'll need to report this data on the Schedule C she'll file with her taxes, but effectively she is now the president of her own company.

Sole Proprietorship	
Description:	The most common type of business structure, the SP is owned by one person and is very easy to set up
Advantages:	Easy and inexpensive to set up; owner is in complete control of the business; profits are taxed only once
Disadvantages:	Potentially unlimited liability for the owner; may be harder to raise capital
How to Set Up:	Choose a name; may need to file a fictitious name application; get an EIN or use your SSN as the EIN

CONCEPT: MINORS AND TAXES

Tax rules change constantly, and the best way to understand current regulations is to check the website of the IRS: www.irs.gov. There is a "threshold" income level – if a minor earns more than that amount, he or she will need to file a return and pay taxes.

During one recent tax year, minors claimed as dependents by a parent or guardian must file their own tax return if they meet any of the following criteria:

• They earned income of greater than $5,800 in the tax year.

• They had unearned income greater than $950. (Unearned income is income from things like interest and dividends.)

- Their net earnings from self-employment were greater than $400 in the tax year.

- Their earned and unearned total income for the year was greater than $950 or their earned income plus $300, whichever is greater.

What kind of protection does an SP provide Kim? Not very much. If one of Kim's customers sues Kim, thinking that she did something that harmed the children she was looking after, that customer could go after not just what Kim's Home Childcare owns, but also everything Kim owns personally (and all the assets of her cosigner/guarantor if she's a minor).

In terms of protection from double taxation, an SP shields you from this. If Kim's company is paid $50 for babysitting services, Kim will pay taxes on that $50 only once, since income generated from an SP is treated as one's personal income.

A sole proprietorship might be a good structure for someone expecting to work alone, from home, in a small start-up business that isn't likely to create much potential liability (e.g., creating a business selling items on eBay is less likely to put you into liability situations than running one that looks after children, sells food, or could injure someone). If your business isn't in that category, you might want to consider one of the business structures described in the next few pages, rather than a sole proprietorship.

General Partnership

A General Partnership, or "GP", is very similar to an SP, but is formed with two or more people. Using the example above, if Kim and her friend Tricia want to form a babysitting company, then KT Childcare is born. Both Kim and Tricia are liable for the company's debts and actions, so if Tricia runs up a bunch of debt and then leaves the company and goes bankrupt, Kim will have to cover all the bills that her partner created. If KT Childcare is sued by an unhappy customer that Kim babysat for, Tricia could lose everything she owns (and her guarantor -- perhaps her parents -- could also lose everything they own) if KT Childcare loses the lawsuit, even though Tricia had nothing to do with that unhappy customer.

It's recommended—required, in some states—that the partnership file a partnership agreement with the county or state where the business is located. The partnership agreement is similar to the operating agreement that we'll look at later.

The partnership will need to create a Schedule K-1 tax form for each partner (which they'll attach to their own tax returns), and partners will file IRS Form 1065 each year. Partners pay taxes on their share of the company's profits.

The GP structure is suitable for a small group of people (generally two to four) who want to set up a business quickly and with minimal cost. The GP is easy to set up, but opens all partners to potentially unlimited liability. Tom and Fred might decide to form a GP if they are going to engage in a narrowly defined business that they don't expect to see large liability risks arising from. For example, they might set up a GP to buy and sell classic stamps or coins by mail.

Tax treatment for a GP is similar to that of an SP – you are subject to double taxation (at the company level and the individual level).

General Partnership	
Description:	Similar to a sole proprietorship, but with two or more owners
Advantages:	Easy and inexpensive to set up
Disadvantages:	Profits taxed once; business profits flow through to the owners' individual tax return; potentially unlimited liability; each partner is responsible for the actions of the others
How to Set Up:	Choose a name; may need to file a fictitious name application; get an EIN or use your SSN as the EIN

Limited Liability Company

A Limited Liability Company, or LLC, is a kind of blend between a GP and a corporation -- you get many of the managerial benefits of a GP, but also much of the protection that a corporation offers. As its name implies, an LLC combines the limited liability of a corporation with the protection from double taxation that a GP provides.

If Kim and Tricia's company, KT Childcare, has a thousand dollars in assets and no liabilities, and the company is sued for ten thousand dollars, the most that Kim and Tricia stand to lose is what the company owns—the thousand dollars. The person suing the company could not, for example, take the company's thousand dollars and also Kim's personal nine-thousand-dollar college savings fund. If the person suing KT Childcare won their suit, Kim and Tricia might decide to pay all they can—one thousand dollars—toward the suit, and then file for bankruptcy.

The LLC structure also allows what is called "pass through" of business earnings to its owners, protecting the partners from double taxation. The owners of an LLC must report business profits or losses on their personal tax returns and file Schedule K-1 returns for all partners.

Setting up an LLC is more time-consuming than setting up an SP or GP, but is not very complicated. Depending on what state you live in, you may need to fill out an LLC Articles of Organization document, which is a simple form that asks for things like the name of the company, purpose of the business, who the "registered agent" for receiving any legal documents is, and the names of the company's members. This will be filed with your secretary of state, and there will be some filing fee (as low as $35 to as high as nearly $1,000), and you may also have to pay a corporate tax at the time you file. You should create an operating agreement, which you will file with your Secretary of State's office. Depending on the state you're in, you may also need to post a notice of the creation of the company in the local newspaper.

LLCs are more complicated and costly to set up than SPs or GPs, but they give business owners significantly more protection. An LLC is a good structure for any company that needs protection from liability and that might grow over time (as it easily allows other members to join). For example, if Charles, Miranda, and Jay were planning on running a pet care business, an LLC might be a good structure for them as it would protect each of them from being sued for accidentally hurting someone's dog or cat.

Limited Liability Corporation (LLC)	
Description:	A partnership in which the owners' liability to most events is limited to the company's assets
Advantages:	Partners' liability is limited; LLC can choose to be taxed either as a partnership or a corporation
Disadvantages:	More difficult and expensive to create than a sole proprietorship of general partnership
How to Set Up:	Submit a copy of your state's LLC Articles of Incorporation to the state; choose a business name; strongly advised that you create and register an Operating Agreement for the business

Corporation

A corporation is a separate legal entity from its owners. In other words, when you incorporate, you're creating a business that will be viewed almost as its own person—something you might be involved with, but which can exist independently of you. Setting up and maintaining a corporation can be much more complex and costly than setting up any other corporate form, but there are unique benefits that come from having this type of structure.

Suppose that Kim and Tricia start KT Childcare as a corporation, "KT Childcare, Inc." (The "Inc." stands for "Incorporated," which is the designation you receive after registering your company as a corporation.) The setup process is more complicated, but at the end of it they might each own half of the company. Kim then leaves the firm, but the company survives. Later, Tricia might depart also, leaving no one at the company, but the company would continue to exist; remember, the corporation is a legal entity that exists independently of its owners. Until someone files paperwork to dissolve and close the company, it continues, and tax returns and other documents need to be prepared and filed each year.

Corporations are good structures for companies that are starting big, or that expect to get big soon. There is no limit to the number of people that can be involved with a corporation (there are limits with an LLC). Also, certain tax benefits are given to corporations that aren't offered to other types of businesses, and the corporation provides the best means of building credit and raising capital for a small- or medium-sized business.

To set up a corporation, you need to create the company's Articles of Incorporation. The contents of these Articles vary from state to state, but they contain basic information such as the corporation's name, address of the headquarters, and the number of shares the corporation will issue (shares are units of ownership of the corporation). You can register your corporation in any state (many people choose Delaware because that state's laws offer more protection to corporations), but you have to file your articles of incorporation in the state your company will be headquartered in. There will be fees, which vary from state to state, that have to be paid to register and file.

Running a corporation can also be more complicated than running a different type of structure: there are more filing requirements and fees; more detailed records required; and the corporation needs to have a board of directors, among other things.

Despite the relative complexity of setting up and running a corporation, and the double taxation that most corporations face (corporations pay tax on the profits they make, and the owners of the corporation must pay taxes on the money they make from the corporation), there are many benefits associated with this type of structure.

Since the corporation is a separate legal entity from its owners and officers, it can build its own credit history and take loans without having individuals co-sign. Credit card companies have designated credit cards just for corporations; investors and banks will generally spend more time with a corporation than with a sole proprietorship or other business type; and some companies won't do business with another firm unless that company is incorporated.

Businesses may choose from a variety of corporate entities based on their needs. Among the types of corporations are the C-Corporation (C-Corp, so-called because it is taxed under Subchapter C of the Internal Revenue Code), S-Corporation (S-Corp, which is taxed under Subchapter S of the Internal Revenue Code), and Professional Corporation (P-Corp, which can only be formed by professionals such as attorneys, engineers, doctors and accountants). We won't go into the details of these different types of corporations; they all share the same basic characteristics of limited liability and are all viewed as "separate entities" from their founders and managers.

Corporations must file an SS-4 Form with the IRS to obtain a tax identification number, which becomes something like the social security number of the business, and will be used to file taxes and create the corporation's own credit profile.

Corporation	
Description:	A corporation is considered a separate legal entity from its founders and owners
Advantages:	Shareholders have limited liability; officers may have more exposure to liability
Disadvantages:	More difficult to set up and expensive to run; profits may be taxed twice; high level of transparency and credibility, making it potentially easier to raise money
How to Set Up:	Create an Articles of Incorporation and file with Secretary of State; register your corporation; strongly suggested you speak with a business attorney when setting up and before selling shares in your business

GETTING PROFESSIONAL HELP

The more complex the business structure, the more likely it is that you'll need to enlist the help of tax experts, attorneys, and other professionals. It's not that difficult to file a tax return for yourself if you're running a sole proprietorship from your bedroom or garage, but you'll definitely want to enlist the help of a professional accountant if you decide to start a corporation.

Tax professionals can save you a lot more than they cost; they can help you with tax savings strategies, business structure issues, and business tax deductions. The good news is that the costs of these "professional fees" can be considered a business expense for your company, so they're tax deductible.

A FINAL WORD ABOUT BUSINESS STRUCTURE

One nice thing about business structures is that you're not married to any particular type. This means that you can start as a sole proprietorship, change to a partnership, then to an LLC, and later to a corporation if you like. Different structures have different appeals to companies in various stages of growth. If you're starting small, you can choose a structure that's easy to set up and manage (a sole proprietorship or LLC, for example) and then change to something more complex (a corporation) later.

Once you know the benefits and drawbacks of each type of business structure and have chosen the one that's best for you, you're ready to start drafting your business plan.

## Chapter 8

Plans for Your Business

THE BUSINESS PLAN

Most experienced businesspeople think that the business plan is the ultimate planning document for a company. In many ways, they're right: the business plan is something that people are used to, and that covers most of the areas that you need to consider when starting a company. The banker considering whether or not to give you a small business loan will know what to expect in one, and will see right away if you've done the work that shows you're serious about your company. It's not the only document or part of the planning process (we'll show you some others later), but it's the most recognized and most popular one, and the plan that's most expected of a serious businessperson.

The business plan has three main functions: to communicate your vision; to track the progress of the business; and to help identify pitfalls and opportunities.

There's no standard template for a business plan, but I've found that the Small Business Administration's (www.sba.gov) business plan format is easy to use and understand, and covers all of the major bases.

My outline for a business plan differs slightly from the SBA's, but there is no set formula for what should and shouldn't be included: you can add or take out sections as you feel necessary. Remember, the objective isn't to create a business plan per se. The plan is a means to an end: the end objective is having a document that communicates the purpose of your business, shows how your business will be successful, tracks the progress of your company, and helps you manage problems and opportunities.

Here are the sections of my business plan template:

1.	The Executive Summary
2.	Company Profile and Identity
3.	Details of the Company
4.	Market Analysis
5.	Team and Organization
6.	Operating Strategy
7.	Financials
8.	Funding Request
9.	Critical Risks
10.	Exit Strategy and Future Plans
11.	Appendixes

Let's look in more detail at how to create each of these sections, starting with the executive summary.

1. The Executive Summary

Imagine that you're a venture capitalist with $500 million to invest in start-up companies. Everyone and their brother is sending you business plans, hoping they'll hit the jackpot and get a couple million of your stash. Each day, you come to work and find a large pile of business plans on your desk -- let's say 100 plans, of 20 pages each, for a total of 2,000 pages. What do you do?

Do you think a VC reads through every plan? One VC I know says he gives ten minutes at most to each plan that comes across his desk. He'll read the first page or two; if something there catches his attention, he'll flip through the rest of the plan in about a minute, checking to see if the financial models are in there, who the key managers are, and so on. Then, he'll either throw it in the trash or put it in the precious "for later reading" pile. About one in 25 plans makes it to that pile and gets more of his time later.

The executive summary (or ES) is your opportunity to catch a person's attention so that they put your plan in their "read later" pile rather than the garbage can. In a few pages, you need to communicate what your business is about, why it can succeed, who's behind it, your funding needs, financial projections, and other key information.

Although it's the first part of your business plan, it should be the last thing you write. Most of what's in the executive summary will be covered in greater detail in other sections of the business plan, and will just be summarized in this section.

Here are some things the executive summary should include:

- A profile of the company, with a mission statement

- The nature of the business and its product/service

- Information on the industry the business is in

- Goals

- Source and use of funds (which can be included elsewhere but alluded to in the ES)

- Financial summary (this can be referred to briefly in the ES and elaborated upon later in the business plan.)

- An exit strategy and/or future plans

We're going to go through each of these areas in more detail. Keep in mind that the ES has to be three things: coherent, concise, and compelling. The ES is a sales document—it's what will "sell" your company or idea to someone else. It needs to catch and hold the interest of the other party. Approach this from a "What's in it for me?" approach, with the "me" being a banker, partner, or other such party. You want to show them that there is a great and unique opportunity available if they are involved with your company in its early stages. You need to convey your passion and enthusiasm, you need to provide a lot of information, and you need to do it in three to four pages.

At the end of your ES, you can include a table of contents, showing the reader where to find detailed descriptions of any area they might be particularly interested in.

We'll come back to the ES at the end of the discussion of the other parts of the business plan. Once we've understood and prepared the other parts of the plan, we can better create a summary hitting key details.

2. *Company Profile and Identity*

<u>A Name</u>

Many novelists say that they don't choose the title of a book until they've finished writing it because they want the book's content to determine the book's name, and not the other way around. While you don't need to actually start a business before you name it, you should pause and think very carefully about your company's identity before choosing a name.

The name of your company is your first step to creating a brand identity. The name should be memorable, should convey the purpose of your business, and should communicate a certain feeling that you are hoping to inspire. Dodge chose the name "Ram" for its series of pickup trucks, and picked the slogan "Dodge trucks are ram tough" to build their truck brand. The word "ram" conveys something powerful, stately, graceful, and rugged. They could just as easily have chosen "Sheep"; but what kind of image would that brand name and identity project?

Ace Hardware is a name that conveys being an expert in the area of hardware. That two-word name creates a positive image in a person's mind, explains what the company does, and puts the name at or near the top of any alphabetical list (such as a phone book's Yellow Pages, which is how many people used to find hardware stores).

Your company's name doesn't even have to be a real word: Zynga and SnapChat are words created by companies to be simple, memorable, and convey a sense of playfulness and accessibility. Netflix is a great example of an imaginary word that explains in seven letters that the company is a movie-through-Internet firm (even though Netflix still does a substantial part of its business through snail mail, the "net" in the name conveyed a sense of something different—a new approach to film delivery).

Here are some steps to use in choosing your company's name. While you are following these steps, also think about slogans or logos that might fit with the company's name.

Let's create a name for a company that does Greek food delivery and catering. First, sit down with a piece of paper and brainstorm on possible names and associations. Write key words that you'd like people to associate with the company: Greek, food, fast, convenient, fresh, affordable, healthy, delicious, friendly, and so on.

After you have written down some name ideas and also some descriptions of how you want people to perceive your business, draw branches from each word with a list of related words. You can use a thesaurus to find some synonyms that might provide the words you're looking for. For example, synonyms for "delicious" might be "tasty," "mouth-watering," "irresistible,""succulent," and "gourmet."

There aren't many synonyms for the word "Greek," but there are many associations: Mediterranean, Athens, gyro, Olympus or Olympian, Socrates, Plato, Zeus, Apollo, Alpha, and a host of words in the Greek language (the Greek words for "meal," "delicious," and so on) that could be used. One thing that springs to my mind when I think Greece is the movie *My Big Fat Greek Wedding;* "My Big Fat Greek Catering Company" would make it on my brainstorming list.

As your list of possible names, related names, and business descriptors grows, start to experiment with different word combinations. By trying different word combinations, names like Gyro Express, Gyros-on-the-Go, Athens Catering, Apollo Caterers, and Plato's Fresh-and-Fast arise.

After you've come up with a list of possible names, check to see if any of them are already being used. You obviously don't want to have a name that's trademarked by someone else or very close to another company's moniker. In my hometown, there was one Thai restaurant named Pad Thai House and another named Pat's Thai House - a situation that caused a lot of problems for the respective owners and their customers. Imagine waiting for your friends at Pad Thai House when they're all waiting for you at Pat's, or being Pat at Pat's Thai House and having to give directions to every fourth person that calls, explaining that you're not the place they're looking for.

After identifying a potential business name, you should check to see if the URL for your business is available. It's a big plus if you can buy the name AppoloCatering.com for your Greek catering company, for use now or in the future (I wouldn't go for that business name, though, because too many people don't know how to spell "Appolo" and might not find the company when searching for it).

You might check quickly to make sure the name translates well. Chevrolet made a famous blunder years ago when it named a car the "Nova," a word that means "no go" in Spanish. You don't want the name of your company to be a profanity in German or Arabic.

A final piece of advice about names: I would avoid names that include your name or names of relatives. Ron Jones Auto Repair may sound fine, until the day an unrelated guy in town named Ron Jones is arrested for pedophilia or running a meth lab in his basement and people start staying away from your body shop.

The last step in the naming process would be to run potential names by people to see what their response is. Ask someone if they can guess what "Apollo Express Foods" does and what feeling the name elicits; ask them if they think "Olympic Catering" conveys more information in a more positive way.

This may sound like a lot of time to be spending on a name, but remember that this is going to be the identity of your company for many people, and for many years.

A Mission Statement

For centuries, different religious groups have sent volunteers abroad to promote their religion's values. These volunteers have historically been referred to as missionaries. Missionaries need to be very clear about their religion's goals and values. They also need to be able to communicate these values in a very succinct and easy to understand way. Mission statements serve a similar purpose in business.

A mission statement is a formal written statement that declares the company's purpose and helps guide its activities, direction, and values. Mission statements should be short, to the point, and clear, but they also need to accurately convey what your business does. This isn't always easy, particularly when the operations of a business are complex or nuanced. It may take a lot of hard work to make sure that your mission statement explains the value your company delivers to the potential customer.

Before writing your own mission statement, look at the mission statements of some successful companies. They are usually not very hard to find since companies want to be very up-front and clear about their mission (you can usually find a company's mission statement by going to their corporate web site and clicking the "About Company" tab). For example, the following four mission statements are publicly available on each company's web site (note: Harley Davidson has two Statements, a Value Statement and a Mission Statement):

Harley Davidson Motorcycles:
We fulfill dreams inspired by the many roads of the world by providing extraordinary motorcycles and customer experiences. We fuel the passion for freedom in our customers to express their individuality.

Starbucks:
Our mission: to inspire and nurture the human spirit – one person, one cup and one neighborhood at a time.

Southwest Airlines:
The mission of Southwest Airlines is dedication to the highest quality of Customer Service delivered with a sense of warmth, friendliness, individual pride, and Company Spirit.

Facebook:
Facebook's mission is to give people the power to share and make the world more open and connected.

All four of these companies are very successful in their respective industries. What do their mission statements have in common? They are all brief and clear, but they are also inspiring. They include words such as freedom, individuality, and spirit. These statements are also customer-centered: They make it very clear that the customer is a priority.

After you draft a company mission statement, be sure that it is clear and informative, but also compare it to the mission statements of the companies above. Does your mission statement reflect a desire to inspire your company to be great? Is your company's purpose clear? Would a potential customer understand your company's identity by reading this mission statement?

The Nature of Your Business

Describing the nature of your business may sound easy: "My friend and I provide math tutoring for grade school kids while we babysit them" or "The company my friends and I are starting puts together birthday parties for kids, with healthy foods and activities."

But sometimes, what seems simple on the surface is actually nuanced and can be complex. "If you're doing tutoring and babysitting, what will you do with my two kids, one of whom is seven and can do simple math problems, but the other of which is only three and is on a different level -- how can you care for both of them and also claim to be teaching them math?" Or "Healthy birthday parties sound great, but how much more expensive will it be to have one than just setting up a bouncy house and baking a cake?" Or, "If I don't offer a sweet birthday cake with lots of icing, won't my kids be disappointed?" This section of your business plan anticipates and responds to these types of questions and concerns, and beefs up your basic business idea.

You should start by answering the most basic questions: What are you selling? Is there a need for it? What things will make your company successful?

You should identify critical success factors and how you will differentiate yourself from competitors. Identify the target market and explain what customers in that market look for when

THE NATURE OF HPK'S BUSINESS

Healthy Parties for Kids ("HPK") is dedicated to offering fun and healthy parties for children between one and fourteen years old. Our target market is parents with kids in this age group, living within a 15-mile radius of downtown, and with a median income level of $75,000. We estimate that there are over 50,000 people who fit this description in our target age group and geography. To us, this means 50,000 opportunities to change the idea of what a birthday party is and what it can offer.

HPK's owners conducted surveys of nearly 100 parents that used our competitors' services for their child's party and found that the following four things were the key decision criteria; they are, therefore, what we believe are the critical success factors for our business:

- **Affordability:** Parents are willing to spend between $15 and $20 per child for a three-hour party.

- **Availability:** It's important that a weekend date near a child's birthday or big event is available.

- **Familiarity:** Parents know what to expect from a party at our established competitors; they have peace of mind knowing that staff are experienced in dealing with kids.

- **Safety and fun:** It is important that the party be held in a safe place, with safe activities, but also that the kids be entertained and enjoy themselves.

Parents indicated that the main things they didn't like about parties at our competitors' were the following:

- **Routine and rush:** Parents feel that their kids are often "rushed out" of a party space in order to make way for the next party, and that there's no individual attention. ("It feels like a party factory, and no one knows or really cares about my kid.")

- **Limited range of food and activities:** Over half of all parents surveyed said that they were fed up with "another pizza and cake" party, or parties in which their kids had access to video games or simply ran around an indoor play area (something they felt wasn't unique or "particularly special").

Our company provides affordable, safe, and fun parties for kids, with special attention devoted to each party and child. We offer a range of healthy foods and fun activities, and our staff engages with the children, using their names, talking about their favorite characters, and giving them quality time and attention. Most parties are held at the parents' home or in public parks, and we encourage outdoor play and activity.

With four founders and a large group of responsible and trained staff and helpers, we are able to offer up to three different parties in three locations at any given date and time, meaning that three kids with the same birthday, wanting parties around lunchtime can all be accommodated—something our competitors, Boingo Gym and Charlie Cheese, can't accommodate and don't manage well (three parties in the same large room means a chaotic mess of kids from different parties "getting lost" in the crowds).

In summary, our competitive advantages are as follows:

- **<u>We are affordable</u>**—nearly twenty percent cheaper than the average competitor.

- **<u>We can accommodate many dates and times</u>**— up to three different parties in three different locations, meaning no "jumble" of kids in one single space.

- **<u>We are familiar</u>**—all of the founders and most of the helpers are students from the local high school. We babysit for the children of many local parents, and people already know and trust us.

- **<u>We offer safe and fun parties</u>**, with a variety of games, activities, and treats.

- **<u>We are not a chain</u>**, but local members of the community that see the kids we entertain in our neighborhoods and communities. We have ties to the community that a franchised business cannot develop.

- **<u>We emphasize customer service and attention</u>**— we know many of the kids we arrange parties for, and we treat each child as unique and special, making particular efforts to use their name and know their age and other things about them.

> • **We address a pressing need in the market, at a key time.** Parents are increasingly concerned about the junk food diets that many kids have access to, and are searching for alternatives. We provide a solution to this problem and answer to these concerns.

deciding to use a product or service like the one you'll offer (the "key decision-making criteria") and how you'll meet those needs.

Keep your explanations broad and general -- there is no need to make long lists of the things you'll sell and the prices for each. Also, keep it simple: Don't entangle the reader in technical jargon or complex processes, thinking you'll impress someone by outlining an elaborate process with lots of details or technical terms usually backfires. The reader should walk away from this section with a very clear idea, elaborated in a couple of sentences, about what need you've identified and will address and what will make you successful.

Let's look at a sample summary for the "healthy birthday party" business idea mentioned earlier (you can find their entire business plan at the end of this book).

This is a good, thorough summary of the nature of HPK's business. In it, the entrepreneurs explained their service, the need for it, the absence of good alternatives, how they're different from their competitors, and the value proposition they offer to parents (low cost + health + peace of mind). They show they've done their homework, having done simple market studies, used questionnaires and surveys, done demographic research on the target market, and identified critical success factors and customer decision-making criteria.

You'll find that much of this summary of the nature of HPK's business is repeated, verbatim, in the executive summary that we'll put together at the end of the business plan. In fact, many of the things you write in the individual sections of the business plan will be restated in the executive summary.

Next, let's look at some of the specific details that should be included in all business plans.

Company Goals

While your mission statement may communicate your broad objectives, you should also clearly state the specific goals of your company. While running a business, it is easy to get off-track, because each day will bring its share of problems, opportunities, and distractions. When opportunities arise, it is important to make sure that you do not deviate from your core business goals. By writing down these goals, understanding them, and committing to them, you will have something to refer to when challenges and opportunities arise.

Consider the case of Harley-Davidson. Given their popularity and loyal customer base, they likely have opportunities every day to launch new product lines that have nothing to do with motorcycles. Their goal may be to build a strong brand that conveys freedom and individuality (see their vision statement in the previous section). By establishing this brand, the company can be seen as unique, and can charge a premium for its product. (Harley may not make the best motorcycle on the market, but it's one of the best brands in the world: How many people do you know that tattoo "Honda," "Coca-Cola," or any other brand onto their bodies?) Their unstated goal might be to make as much money as possible, but they view the building and maintenance of their brand as the best way of achieving that goal over the long term. So, if a company approached Harley-Davidson about using their name for a kid's cereal, they'd probably turn it down because it's not consistent with the brand image they want to maintain, even though passing up this opportunity would lead to less profit in the near term.

The lesson here is to understand the relationship between your identity and your goals, both short-term and long-term. Sometimes, you might have an opportunity that enhances your business in the near term, but could damage its viability over the long term. Short-term profits at Goldman Sachs, for example, caused the company a lot of damage to its reputation (its "brand"), as the company was seen by many as one of the profiteers of the financial crisis of 2007-2008.

Something that will help you in setting goals is classifying them as short-, intermediate-, or long-term ones. You can then evaluate a potential transaction for its impact on all three categories of goals (i.e., "it helps in the short-term, is slightly negative in the mid-term, and potentially destructive in the long-term").

Goals will also help keep your company on track, focusing on priorities and striving to achieve certain milestones in a defined period of time. Ambiguous goals, such as "being the best caterer in town" aren't as meaningful as more specific, measurable ones, such as "being the number one caterer in the county as measured by revenues, and having a customer satisfaction score of eighty-five percent or above." Not all goals need to have numbers attached to them: "Be the number one furniture delivery company in the city as measured by revenues by the time we finish college" is a measurable goal that is more credible than "Have $117,239.18 in revenues in three years."

If you're the leader of a start-up company with a few people involved, you should get "buy in" from other people regarding the goals. People, whether partners or employees, will feel more committed to a goal if they've had a hand in setting it. Similarly, different people should be assigned different goals and given some responsibility over the handling of means to achieve those objectives.

For example, in the case of Apollo Express Foods, one person might be in charge of the goal "secure three large ($10,000-plus) annual corporate contracts within three months of start-up" (a sales and marketing job), whereas someone else might be in charge of the goal "ensure that 95 percent or more deliveries arrive within twenty minutes of promised times" (an operational goal). Remember, one key role of a leader is delegating responsibility, and not trying to micromanage every part of the business.

By assigning tasks, the business leader can better hold people accountable for failures, or reward them for successes.

SMART Goals

A helpful approach to writing your company's goals is to follow SMART criteria. This analytical framework helps you to always make sure that your goals are Specific, Measurable, Attainable, Relevant, and Time-Bound.

Specific:

While you want your mission statement to be a general statement of your company's purpose, you want your goals to specifically state what you will do. For example, one of your first short-term goals that is very specific could be to "create a budget." A mid-term goal might be "sign a lease on a store site by month six."

Measurable:

There is no use having a goal when there is no way to determine if it has been met. The goal should be worded in a way that explicitly states how you track progress towards the objective. For example, if your goal is to grow your business, you will not really be able to tell if you've met this goal unless you include a numerical target for your business growth. The goal "grow revenues by twenty-five percent in year two" is easier to measure than the goal "grow the business."

Attainable:

Setting a goal that is attainable yet ambitious may be a tricky balancing act. You should not make the mistake of setting unrealistic goals. You need to be honest about what you can realistically expect to achieve. If you decide to start a fast food company, the goal "surpass McDonald's in annual revenue" is probably not an attainable one.

Setting lofty goals can seem like a good motivational strategy, but if you continually fail to hit your targets, you and your team will start to feel dejected. Be realistic and set goals that you have the means to achieve. "Deliver a hamburger that consistently beats the Big Mac in taste tests and sells for 10 percent less" could be an attainable goal.

Relevant:

Make sure that you are setting appropriate objectives for your business. You can easily envision how a Starbucks executive, given that company's mission statement, might set the following goal: "Change the everyday attitude of our customers by making them more positive, optimistic people." A mission like this sounds nice, but isn't really relevant for a coffee company.

The mission of Starbucks may be ambitious and utopian, but their goals must remain relevant. Starbucks makes and sells coffee. Therefore, their goals should be relevant to their core business. "Play, promote, and sell music that enhances the coffee-drinking and 'third place' experience; sell 50,000 CDs per month by the end of December" could be an appropriate and relevant goal—something not directly related to coffee, but to enhancing the customer experience.

Time-Bound:

This is perhaps the easiest criterion to understand, but it is often neglected. When writing your goals, be sure to specify a date or timeline by which you intend to achieve them. One way to make sure that your goals are time-bound is to classify them into time-based groups, such as three-month goals, six-month goals, and twelve-month goals (you can also make short-, mid-, and long-term goals). Alternatively, you can specify a date by which you intend to achieve each goal. This is helpful because you can always refer to your timeline to remind yourself of what you set out to accomplish in a given time period.

By setting SMART goals, you will ensure that you rally the company around things you believe are important to achieve. In other words, before you become overwhelmed by the everyday mayhem of running a business, you will have well-thought-out goals that are clear, realistic, and are written in a way that holds you or your employees accountable.

Finally, next to each goal you may wish to specify your strategy (or tactic) for achieving that objective. In some cases, the strategy may be obvious and may not even need to be stated, however, it is good practice to specify how you plan to achieve each goal. By writing out each strategy, you will have a task list that you can refer to and check off when each goal is accomplished. This is a great way to stay on track, avoid forgetting important jobs, and even report your progress to investors or funders.

Here's what the founders of Healthy Parties for Kids have set as their goals.

GOALS FOR HPK, LLC

Immediate (next one to four weeks):

- Complete business plan and approach bank for a business loan
- Register company with Secretary of State
- Obtain EIN and set up bank accounts

Near-Term (next three to six months):

- Create promotional material and distribute at "Springfield Kids Fair" in January
- Sign up 25 new customers
- Finish web site creation and testing

Mid-Term (next 12-24 months):

- Obtain bank or other loan to purchase delivery truck
- Sign partnership agreement with health food company for cross-promotion and joint purchasing
- Begin expansion into teen- and corporate-party business areas

Long-Term (three to five years):

- Generate 25 percent of revenues from non-children's parties
- Begin expansion into "pre-made" healthy meal segment (HPK makes healthy meals for kids, and strategic partner sells in their stores)
- Begin process of franchising the business

Goal setting is a key step that most small start-ups neglect or don't do well. If you're setting up a business on your own and don't plan to have partners, employees, or need financing from banks or investors, you may think that the time spent making your goals would be better spent just acting—starting the business and making the plan as you go.

A lot of businesspeople rationalize that the business environment changes so fast that goals and plans, especially long-term ones, are made irrelevant. They ask themselves: *"What's the sense of making a long-term goal for a business that hasn't been started yet, in a business environment that changes so quickly that I'll probably have to change all my goals many times just in the first few months?"*

Your goals will help you on track and allow you to measure your progress, as well as highlight areas that you need to work harder at and those in which you can ease off the gas. They will demonstrate to others that you have put the necessary preparation and thought into your business to increase its chances of success. They'll crystallize ideas so that others can buy into a concrete vision with quantifiable and measurable results. They'll help keep you focused on the task at hand, enhancing your sense of achievement and company morale as employees check off one goal successfully achieved and move their attention to the next.

Finally, remember that your business plan is a living document; it's not something you write and put on the shelf forever. It's something that you should come back to again and again to modify based on changes in the marketplace, the current business environment, and other circumstances. In a similar manner, you may come back to your long-term goals a year after startup and decide to rewrite all of them. That's perfectly fine. Having goals, putting them on paper, and doing your best to attain them is more important than the specific goal itself.

3. *Details of the Company:*

This section of your business plan gives the reader a more detailed description of your business, including key details about its form, location, key dates, and other information.

Things you should include in this section are

- Registered name
- The company's mission statement
- The date business began or is expected to begin
- The legal form of the business, or business structure
- Ownership
- Names and roles of key members

It may also include things like

- Milestones achieved to date
- Description of the product or service
- History of the idea or current business
- New potential growth areas
- Any other factual data that can be concisely repre-sented and that you deem useful to the reader

This is a fairly easy part of the plan to write, since it's mostly short, bullet-pointed factual information. It doesn't have to be flowery or persuasive; it is just meant to fill in some details for the reader.

Here's an example of the company detail section for HPK Company:

COMPANY DETAILS, HPK, LLC

Registered Name:
Healthy Parties for Kids, LLC
Date of Formation:
January 1
Company Legal Form:
Delaware Limited Liability Corporation
Company Ownership and Paid-In Capital:
Trinity, President, 20%, $500
Jordan, Director of Sales and Marketing, 20%, $500
Logan, Director of Operations, 20%, $500
Bailey, Director of Finance, 20%, $500
Other Paid-In Capital, 20%, $1,000

Company Mission Statement and Vision:

Healthy Parties for Kids is dedicated to improving the health of children and easing the burdens of busy parents by organizing and hosting healthy and enjoyable gatherings for young people.

Key Milestones Achieved To Date:

- Market study and competitive analysis
- Customer Needs survey of over 100 parents
- Organization of over a dozen events for target audience
- Revenue of over $4,000 in the past six months
- Drafting of business plan
- Formation of LLC
- Social marketing campaign launch

4. Market Analysis

This section will identify the industry you're in, show that you understand the dynamics of it, and explain the opportunities within the industry. You should include data such as statistics, findings from market studies, numbers regarding the size and growth of the industry, and some analysis of your company's position vis-à-vis its competitors.

Some of the preliminary analysis was done in the "idea stage" of the process, when you did your SWOT and Porter's Five Forces Analyses. These types of analyses should be enhanced by preliminary and basic market research (such as polls or questionnaires of potential customers to assess their needs and priorities) and some analysis of specific competitors.

Here are some things you can address in this section:

- Your target market
- Characteristics of your target market (critical needs, demographic information, geographic location)
- The size of the market (the number of potential customers, the frequency of purchases, expected growth in the market)
- Your ability to get market share, and how you'll be able to do that (how you'll win business from established competitors)
- Pricing and profit expectations and trends
- How you will reach your target audience
- Purchasing cycles of the target market
- Competitive analysis and barriers to entry

Here's the Market Analysis section of HPK's business plan.

HPK'S MARKET ANALYSIS

Industry Size, Growth, and Trends:

In the last 50 years, a typical eight-year-old's birthday party has changed from a gathering of five to ten friends at the child's home, with a few games (Pin the Tail on the Donkey, Twister) and cake being served, to large and elaborate gatherings of 100 people or more, with paid entertainers, bouncy houses, ponies, and a variety of themes. The increase in single-parent households and households in which both parents work has created a need for convenience, as many moms and dads today do not have the time to plan and run a party for their children, yet remain committed to the idea of giving their young ones a memorable event.

Background data on our industry is very favorable for HPK:

- The children's birthday party market in the U.S. is estimated to be a $10 billion industry, and one that has grown by over 10 percent a year over the last decade. (Author's note: all of these data are fictional; when you do cite statistics and data, you will need to cite sources of those.)

- Billings Research estimates that the kid's party industry will grow to over $20 billion in the next five years, as busy parents increasingly "outsource" the planning and hosting of children's parties to outside vendors.

- The average outside party cost for a child has risen from less than $100 ten years ago to over $250 currently, according to Vector Party Research.

- There was no noticeable decline in party spending for kids during the economic recession of 2007–2008.

- Demographics are favorable, with nearly 20 million people moving into our target market over the next three years.

The Local Industry and Competitors:

- There are 17 party planners in the city, but none focus on young kids.
- There are three established companies that regularly host parties for kids.
- Competitors' costs are higher than HPK's, capacity is limited, and many parents are tired of their "routine."

Our research finds 17 companies that are active in party arrangement in our city. None of these companies focuses exclusively on children, and over half are geared toward weddings and office parties.

Three companies that do regularly host birthday parties for children in our area—Charlie Cheese Pizza, Boingo Gym, and Carl's Bowling and Arcade—do a brisk business. Our observations over a two-month period indicate an average of seven parties a day on Saturday and Sunday, with average attendance of fourteen people and an average total price of $425, for an average per weekend revenue of nearly $6,000 per location.

Discussions with managers at these businesses reveal that the birthday business has grown between 20 and 30 percent for each company in the last two years, and is expected to continue growing at a similar rate for the foreseeable future.

Our Target Market:

- Parents with children between one and fourteen years old

- Families within a 15-mile radius of downtown
- Relatively affluent, with median income of $75,000 per household
- Approximately 50,000 kids in our target market
- New market opportunity: Many parents choose to have parties at home because they don't appreciate the junk food and cookie-cutter nature of parties at other locations; we can tap this market of health-and-fitness-conscious parents who "want something different" in their child's birthday party.

Our Positioning and Competitive Advantage:

HPK's owners conducted surveys of nearly 100 parents that used our competitors' services for their child's party and found that the following four things were their key decision criteria and what we believe are our critical success factors:

- <u>Affordability:</u> Parents are willing to spend between $15 and $20 per child for a three-hour party.

- <u>Availability:</u> It's important that a weekend date near a child's birthday or big event is available.

- <u>Familiarity:</u> Parents know what to expect from a party at our established competitors; they have peace of mind knowing that staff are experienced in dealing with kids.

- <u>Safety and fun:</u> It is important that the party be held in a safe place, with safe activities, but also that the kids be entertained and enjoy themselves.

a. Competitive Positioning

	HPK	Charlie Cheese	Boingo Gym	Adam's Arcade
"Basic Package" Average Cost (20 kids, 10 parents)	$ 350.00	$ 435.00	$ 425.00	$ 405.00
Cost of Facilities, food & other	Included	$ 385.00	$ 375.00	$ 355.00
Cost of cake, invitations & other	Included	$ 50.00	$ 50.00	$ 50.00
# of parties that can be held at one time	3	5	1	2
# of Themes Available	5	1	1	1
# of Activities Available	37	1	2	2
# of Menu Items	75	8	4	15

	HPK	Charlie Cheese
Average Party Cost	$ 350.0	$ 435.0
Cost of Facilities, food, etc	Included	$ 385.0
Cost of cake, invitations, etc	Included	$ 50.0
# of parties that can be held	3	5
# of Themes	5	1
# of Activities	37	1 (arcade)
# of Menu Items	75	8
Familiarity	Founders and employees are members of community and babysit for parents	Well-known national brand
Strengths	Affordable, safe, convenient, unique, healthy, personal attention to kids, health & fitness appeal	Brand, predictability, can hold many parties simultaneously
Weaknesses	Lack of brand awareness	Chaotic Unhealthy Kids get little personal attention
Opportunities	Appeal to people that throw own parties because they can't afford or don't like the "corporate" party feel Easy to expand -- large labor pool; easy to train new hires	
Threats	Low barriers to entry	

Prior to launching the business, the four founders organized and ran over a dozen birthday parties with a total of over 250 attendees. Feedback was very positive in every event, and testimonials can be found in the appendix, along with sample marketing materials (fliers and a snapshot of our web page), and a menu of different party options (themes, activities, treats, etc.).

b. Other Opportunities, Purchase Patterns, and Market Access

- There is a large potential market of parents who host their own parties because they want the party to be at home, don't like "corporate" kid's parties, and want their kids to have more individual attention. Our competitors cannot tap this market.
- We could potentially expand to healthy office parties, corporate events, and high school events (i.e., dances, parties).
- Birthdays occur only once a year, but parents who choose to use a competitor like Charlie Cheese one year aren't likely to return the next year (they want to provide a variety of experiences for their child); HPK can expect significant repeat business, as our parties are distinct from one another and customizable (two parents that we hosted parties with during our "trial period" have already asked us to organize parties for their other kids).
- We have good access to the market through community, church, and school involvement. We have a network of kids we regularly babysit for, and plan to send public relations letters to local newspapers and television news. We run a blog about our parties and have over 20,000 followers on Twitter.

5. Team and Organization

As an entrepreneur, you have the opportunity to do something that many business managers would envy: you get to decide how to structure your organization, who will be involved, and whom to hire.

If and when your business moves from being one run by a single person to one involving, potentially, many people, you will need to create a framework for organizing and managing the people in your company. If you start up with friends, you should determine early on the roles and responsibilities each person in the company will have.

In the business plan, you should highlight different key members of your company, providing background on them and explaining their roles. You should also provide some information about how the key members or founders know one another. For younger people, without much work experience, highlight any relevant experience you do have and the characteristics that are relevant to your role. You could also include your résumé(s) in the appendix of the business plan.

Things from this section to include in the Business Plan

- Names and roles of key company members
- Ownership information
- Background on the relationship between the founders
- Explanation of how decisions are made (the organizational structure) and who's responsible for what

a. Ownership

You can elect to put information about the ownership of the company and capital invested in it. Keep in mind that not all contributions are equal. In other words, suppose that both you and your father put $500 of "paid-in capital" into your company. The dollar amount invested shouldn't reflect company ownership: even though you each put in 50 percent of the company's paid-in capital, you might be doing all the work while your dad is just a silent investor, so you might own 75 percent of the business, while your dad gets the other 25 percent.

You need to negotiate ownership interest based on things like the amount of money a person is investing in the business; time he or she willl contribute and work they'll do; and equipment or other contributions they'll make to the company. If a friend is letting your business use his pickup truck and tools, you need to determine how much he should receive for that, and if the payment should be simply an expense (paid in cash) or will be given in the form of ownership in the firm.

b. Organizational Structure

You should also consider including an organizational structure in this section of your business plan. An organizational structure is simply a structure that shows the decision-making path within a company and notes who is involved in the process. Let's look at two common forms of management structures at start-ups, and the plusses and minuses of each.

A democratic, or "flat," structure is one in which all of the people in the business are equal to one another. Decisions are made by consensus or majority vote.

The main benefit of this type of organizational structure is that people in the business feel valued—they feel that their opinions count, and they have a sense of empowerment because they can make and implement decisions.

The main negative of this structure is that "flat" works in theory, but rarely in practice, particularly for larger organizations. Politics enter the scene (e.g., one partner makes a deal with another: "I'll vote with you on this item if you promise to vote with me on the next one"). Also, people may feel that they have more knowledge of a particular issue than their colleagues do, and resent that their vote is being cancelled out by someone "who doesn't know anything about the subject."

Flat structures are usually the "default" of many small start-ups. That is, start-ups that don't spend time planning or organizing typically "assume" that the structure is flat and that all major decisions will be made by agreement amongst the founders. Typically, these companies are set up by a couple or a few good friends, and it's assumed that the unwritten dynamics of the friendship will solve all eventual problems (e.g., "John's good with numbers, so it's natural he's the finance guy, whereas I found our first customers, so I guess I'm the salesperson, and we just talk through all the big decisions together").

That might sound good internally, for the company and the people in it who know each other well, but it's not really a process that can be understood easily by someone not familiar with you (and remember, the business plan's purpose is to communicate key information, such as how the team makes decisions, to outsiders). Also, I've found that the decision-making "process" falls apart fairly easily, and can create major rifts in the company. For example, one partner takes out a big part of the company's profits to buy himself a car; the other partners get upset because they thought the money should be used to grow the business, but the partner that took the money out views it as his to do with as he pleases.

Flat structures can work, but roles and responsibilities need to be explained and put in writing up front. An operating agreement (discussed later) should be in place.

An alternative to the flat structure is an autocracy, or "top-down" structure. This structure has one person at the top and the other people below him or her. For example, there might be a president, with two vice presidents (such as a VP of Finance and a VP of Marketing) below the president.

The main benefit of this structure is that someone who has a good knowledge of the company can make decisions quickly. It's also clear who's in charge of the company and the different critical functions, so people can be held accountable, and the "expert" in one area will have more control of decisions in his or her department.

There are negatives to the top-down structure, though. If more than one person started the business, the person not in charge may resent the unequal partnership. A good leader possesses a broad array of skills; if the head of the company is lacking in some key areas, he or she can make decisions that are very harmful to the business.

A Typical Top-Down Organizational Structure

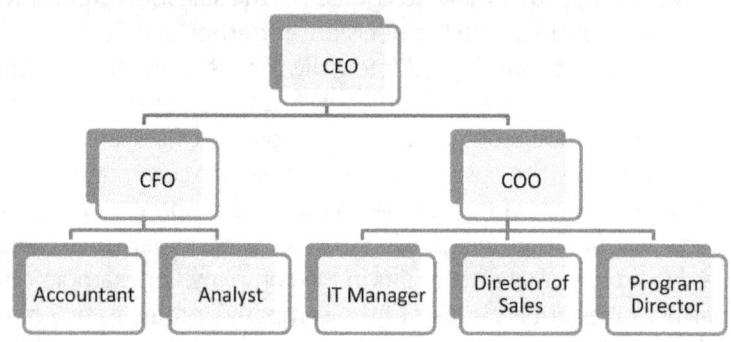

This is a typical structure for a larger organization. For small start-ups, it's a structure that generally comes about after the business grows to four or more people.

Potential Pitfalls with Creating Your Organization:

A few key problem areas in organizing your team that you should be aware of and avoid:

1. **The person who founded the business may not be the best person to run it.** Just because someone came up with a business idea or started the company doesn't mean she should run it. She might be better in a more focused role (i.e., running a division or function) than in the diverse role of business leader. You shouldn't automatically place the person who came up with the business idea at the top of the company.

2. **There should be mechanisms for changing the people in key positions without destroying or seriously disrupting the company.** If Jason is the head of the company but makes terrible investment decisions, it should be possible and not fatally disruptive for June or Gareth to replace him as the president, removing him entirely from the company if need be, or at least moving him to an area where his talents can help the firm.

3. **Sometimes new people are more trouble than they're worth.** If your business is running efficiently but you want to expand and are considering hiring someone, you need to think about all the "mental capital" (time and effort) of yours that person is going to consume. Particularly if you're younger, hiring another

   17-year-old to come into your business might entail a lot of time and frustration "directing" that person.

   Older, more experienced people are usually more able to direct themselves (but less likely to let a "kid" give them orders); if you hire a younger person with the expectation that the person is as motivated, smart, and hardworking as you and your partner, you might be very disappointed to find that you're spending half your time just telling him what he needs to do and getting little productive work out of your new employee.

   Don't be anxious to grow your business too soon: Bootstrap -- do the work yourself until you honestly cannot do more -- and then choose your hires very carefully. You might want to consider "hiring" a parent or adult friend to help part-time, which could be much more productive than hiring a teen full-time.

4. **Doing business with friends?** There are two schools of thought on this topic: 1) Never do business with friends, as the non-business relationship could lead to poor business decisions

and the friendship could be strained or destroyed by disputes related to the business; 2) Do business with friends because you know them better than other people and you can trust them.

Personally, I am in the latter group. I prefer working with people I respect, know well, and trust, and these people are oftentimes my friends. I would say this, however: while I think that starting a business with a friend or friends isn't a bad idea, I would avoid hiring friends as the business grows. Being an "equal" with your friend in the business is one thing; being their boss is another, and the mixing of the business and friend relationship is a volatile one. *Partner* with people you know well and trust (who are usually friends); *hire* the best-qualified person for the job (usually, they're not your friends).

There are many types of organization structures: virtual, network, functional, divisional, geographical, and so on. The important thing isn't necessarily what type of structure to have, but having a structure in the first place. Outline in writing each person's roles and responsibilities, how decisions are made, how people are added and removed, and other areas. Much of this will be explained in the chapter dealing with the operating agreement.

Here is HPK's explanation of their team and structure:

HPK'S ORGANIZATIONAL STRUCTURE

Our business was formed and is run by four high school friends who have grown up together. We have years of experience in dealing with children through our babysitting jobs, and have tested the kid-party planning idea for over six months.

Executives and Key Personnel

The founders and key members of the Company are as follows:

Trinity, President

Trinity is a senior at Springfield High School. She is the student body vice president, a cheerleader, and a member of the honor society. Trinity spent two years working for Daddy Day Care of Springfield, helping to organize teaching curriculum, ordering supplies and equipment, making meals, and working with other staff. She has been a babysitter in the community for nearly five years, and a volunteer with Habitat for Humanity for two years. Trinity sets the strategic direction of the Company, and is involved in all key aspects of decision-making.

Jordan, Director of Sales and Marketing

Jordan became interested in sales and marketing three years ago when she started working with Big Jim's Catering, helping the owner identify and sign new catering clients. Jordan has helped local businesses create and manage web sites to advertise their services, and has advised two companies on Internet marketing strategies. She is a senior at Springfield High School.

Logan, Director of Operations

Logan has spent three years working at Salad Express, where he is an assistant manager. He has experience with supplier relations, inventory control, deliveries and catering, cooking procedures, and employee management. He is a senior at Springfield High School, and a member of the Business Club.

Bailey, Director of Accounting and Finance

Bailey is a junior at Springfield High School, where she serves as class treasurer and is a member of the Business Club. Her interest in accounting and finance came from her parents, who run a small business and have taught her the basics of bookkeeping, accounting, and finance. She has worked on the financials of the family business, a coffee shop and deli, for the past four years.

Kelly, Business Advisor

Kelly, Bailey's mother, is an accomplished businesswoman who has set up and run two successful food-service businesses, Kelly's Bagels and Kelly's Coffee & Cake, both of Springfield. Kelly advises the Company on key management and operational issues. She is a member of the Springfield Restaurant Association, Springfield Chamber of Commerce, Springfield School Board, and Springfield Community Church. She won the coveted "Best Businesswoman" award from the Springfield Chamber of Commerce in 2004.

Relationship of the Founders

The founders of the company grew up together in Springfield, attending elementary, junior high, and high school together. They have a strong and long-lasting friendship, and have worked together in other business ventures (a babysitting business). The founders have complementary skills and talents, and work well together.

The Ownership of the Company

Ownership of the Company is as follows:

Name	Role	Paid-In Capital	% Ownership
Trinity Adams	Co-Founder	$ 500.00	20.0%
Jordan Logas	Co-Founder	$ 500.00	20.0%
Ariel Miller	Co-Founder	$ 500.00	20.0%
Bailey Lee	Co-Founder	$ 500.00	20.0%
Kelly Lee	Advisor	$ 500.00	15.0%
Kyle Lee	Investor	$ 500.00	5.0%
Total		$ 3,000.00	100.0%

The Future of the Team

All of the team members plan to remain in Springfield following their graduation from high school, allowing us to continue working together to grow our business after graduation.

The résumés of all founders can be found in the Appendixes.

Operating Strategy

This section explains the broader strategy for implementing the business plan. This section covers a few key areas, and any specifics should be consistent with sales, costs, and other assumptions made in the financials section.

The operations strategy section should address the following broad areas:

- Sales and marketing strategy
- Growth strategy
- Production plan
- Personnel plan

Not every business needs to address each of the above areas, and of course you can add areas if you think they are important to your business. The important thing is that you communicate what the key strategies and tactics are for each relevant area of your company.

a. The Marketing Strategy

This section needs to explain how you will find and create customers. How will you identify potential customers and communicate with them? How will you build your brand, create trust in the firm, and generate repeat business? How will you communicate with other groups? How will you distribute your product or service?

This section can include information about advertising methods, promotional tactics, customer retention and satisfaction strategies, and other issues.

b. The Growth Strategy

How will your company grow and expand? Will it hire more people, open another store, acquire a competitor, move from the garage to renting manufacturing space, franchise, or add new products?

There are essentially two ways to grow your business. They're known as "organic" and "inorganic."

Organic growth is natural growth that comes from increases in a business's activity. It comes from adding more people, more stores, more factories, or other input factors.

Inorganic growth is growth that comes through acquiring another company or merging with another business.

If Southwest Airlines buys a bunch of new planes and adds a number of new routes, that's considered organic growth; if Delta and Southwest Airlines merge to form a much larger airline, that's considered inorganic growth.

It's most likely that for the first few years of your business your growth will be organic. That doesn't mean that the growth has to be slow or capital-intensive, though. If you own a good business and franchise it, it's possible to see explosive growth by recruiting people to follow your business model and run local franchises of your company.

c. The Production Plan

How will you produce the product? Where? How much of the production process will you do on your own, and which parts will be outsourced? Who are the key suppliers? How much inventory do you need?

d. The Personnel Plan

How many employees are there? What special qualifications or training do they need? How large is the labor pool? How do you find and keep good personnel? What are your personnel needs going forward, and have you identified people to fill these roles?

HPK's Operations Strategy looks like this:

HPK'S OPERATIONS STRATEGY

Marketing and Sales Strategy

HPK has a multifaceted approach to marketing our services:

- **Web-based marketing:** The Company has a web site that allows customers to get information on our services, read testimonials from satisfied customers, print coupons, and get more information. We use social media actively to promote our business, and we have a website and blog. We are well reviewed on online review sites.
- **Word of mouth and referral:** Anyone who refers us to a person that becomes a customer receives a $20 savings bond in their child's name. We offer a 10 percent discount on any repeat business.
- **Print advertising:** The Company has posted fliers on the bulletin boards of the YMCA, area churches, the library, and other places where parents with young children assemble. We are speaking with the PTAs of two elementary schools about distributing information to their members. In the future, the company anticipates advertising in *Springfield Parents Magazine.*
- **PR:** The Company has a public relations strategy, mailing press releases to local newspapers and television news stations (see Appendix).

- **Other:** The Company is negotiating with a local health food store about the prospect of the store "sponsoring" our business—providing food and drinks to the Company at heavily discounted prices in return for our company advertising the store at our events and on our web site.

Personnel Plan:

The Company regularly hires high school students the founders know to assist on an as-needed basis, with competitive hourly pay. The average party requires only one to two people to plan, host, and clean up, so personnel in addition to the four managers are only required if more than two parties are being held at the same time on a given date. In every case, our Company has a minimum of two, and an average of four, weeks advance notice about the details of the party -- ample time to source additional personnel, if necessary.

Growth Strategy:

HPK anticipates handling an average of 10 parties a week by the end of one year of operations. By the end of the first year, we anticipate hiring and training two to three additional employees, and increasing the offering of products by branching into teen (Sweet 16 parties, proms) and corporate events (store openings, office parties). In the long term, we believe there is the potential to franchise the business.

Financials

Financial planning is one of the most critical requirements for business, and having a set of good financial statements can be the difference between success and failure for many companies. If you think your business might need to raise capital from a bank, vendor, supplier, investor or partner, a solid set of financial statements can be invaluable. Unfortunately, many businesspeople are so intimidated by financial statements that they neglect making them, or pay big bucks to someone else for doing what the company's founding members should have already done.

Making financial statements is not difficult. It doesn't require expertise in accounting or higher math, and by taking the time to make the financials yourself, you'll learn to speak the language of people in the finance industry. The bank loan officer or venture capitalist you might meet with to evaluate a funding request from your company will be impressed that you know the numbers behind your business.

a. The Importance of Financial Statements

Even if you don't anticipate showing your statements to someone else, your financial statements will have a tremendous internal value.

I know many entrepreneurs who didn't make financial statements or do any financial analysis of their business until it was too late. It's not uncommon to see someone who seems to be running a very good business but who never gets ahead. He or she works around the clock, has a large group of loyal customers, and seems to be doing a brisk business, but when you talk to them they explain that they "don't know where all the money is going" and wonder how they can be selling so much but seeing so little profit.

There are even businesspeople who think they're making money on each sale but who are, in fact, losing money with every transaction. These people usually end up shutting down their business or going to a professional who does the same type of financial analysis that you will learn to do in this chapter.

b. Don't Be Intimidated

What you'll see in this section is a set of detailed financial statements made on Microsoft Excel, a spreadsheet program. If you don't know what a spreadsheet is or how to use Excel, don't worry: your financial statements don't have to be made on a computer or with a spreadsheet program; you can write the basic information in a notebook if you like.

Spreadsheet programs like Excel aren't that difficult to learn, and they make things like adding rows of numbers a lot easier than writing the figures on a piece of paper and using a calculator. If you don't know how to use Excel or don't have access to a PC, the concepts and information you'll get from this chapter will still be very useful.

You don't necessarily need to make your financial plans as detailed as the ones in this chapter. The statements we'll look at soon are very detailed ones, made to show you what a really thorough set of financials would look like. You can make your statements much more basic, if you like, as long as they cover the same general areas (how much you are expecting to sell, how much your costs are expected to be, and how much profit the business will make).

Don't be intimidated by Excel spreadsheets with lots of numbers in small print on them. You will learn how to make and read these things, and you can then decide how much detail your company does or doesn't need and if you'd like to make the effort to put them into Excel or not.

c. What Types of Financial Statements Do You Need to Have?

There are three main statements that we'll go through in detail. You'll find that these statements are used in nearly every kind of business, of every size, all over the world. So if you get familiar with them, the knowledge can help you not only in your own company, but at any company you might work for, invest in, or partner with.

The P&L

The first of the "Big Three" financial statements is the income statement, or P&L (profit and loss) statement. The P&L shows revenues and costs: Money coming into and going out of the business. What's left over after all costs (including taxes) is your net income or net profit. (In finance, "gross" means "before adjustments" and "net" means "after everything.")

Let's take the case of Coffee Catering, a company started by two high school friends and their two older brothers. Coffee Catering delivers coffee and breakfast foods for morning meetings at companies, conference rooms, and other places. The business was set up in December and started operating the following January.

To make a P&L for Coffee Catering, we need to know the following:

1. What are the main sources of sales? For Coffee Catering, there are two main items, beverages and food.
2. What are the costs? This is where it gets a little more complicated. There are direct costs, known as Costs of Goods Sold (COGS) and indirect costs (such as

advertising, utility, and travel costs). COGS are the costs that Coffee Catering has to pay in order to run their business; the indirect costs are known as Sales, General, and Administrative (or SG&A).

a. COGS for Coffee Catering: the cost of food; the cost of beverages; the costs of labor, rent, insurance, supplies, truck rental, and gas

b. SG&A for Coffee Catering: marketing expenses, sales expenses, and depreciation (which we'll look at later)

If you add up the direct and indirect costs of operating the business, you'll have Coffee Catering's total operating costs.

Taking the total revenue of the company and subtracting the operating costs from it will give you the company's operating profit (or loss).

For example, if Coffee Catering sells $100 in beverages and $150 in food, then its total sales, or total revenue, will be $250. If the operating costs were $150, then the company has made an operating profit of $100.

There are a few "non-operating" items that we'll want to include in the P&L: the first will be "interest income and other."

If the company has cash in a savings account and earns interest on this, we'll put that figure in this area. If the company sells an old coffee maker for $20, we'll include that as "other" income in this line of the P&L, since selling equipment isn't part of the company's operating business. We'll include a line called "interest expense and other" to account for interest the company has to pay or other non-operating expenses (actually, you should break down your non-operating income and expenses into more categories, but we want to keep things simple at this point).

Finally, there are taxes. Coffee Catering will set aside 30 percent of their profits before taxes to cover the tax bill. What's left after all that is known as the company's net profit or loss.

Here, then, are the simplified formulas:

- Total Sales minus COGS = Gross Profit
- Gross Profit minus SG&A = Operating Profit
- Operating Profit plus Interest Income and Other Income, minus Interest Expense and Other Expenses = Profit Before Taxes
- Profit Before Taxes minus 30% (for taxes) = Net Profit or Loss

Here's what Coffee Catering's P&L looks like for their first month of operations, January:

A Monthly P&L for Coffee Catering

Income Statement for Coffee Catering	January
Total Sales	**$ 1,098.00**
Food Sales	$ 415.00
Beverage Sales	$ 683.00
COGS (direct costs)	**$ 536.20**
Food Materials	$ 103.75
Beverage Materials	$ 102.45
Labor	$ -
Rent	$ 100.00
Insurance	$ 50.00
Supplies	$ 80.00
Truck Rental	$ 100.00
Gross Profit	**$ 561.80**
SG&A	**$ 140.00**
Marketing	$ 75.00
Sales Expenses	$ 40.00
Depreciation	$ 25.00
Operating Profit	**$ 421.80**
Interest Income and other	$ 10.00
Interest Expense and other	$ 50.00
Earnings before taxes	**$ 381.80**
Taxes (30% est)	$ 114.54
Net Profit/(Loss)	**$ 267.26**

You might notice that there's no labor expense. Most entrepreneurs don't pay themselves a salary or wage, but rather take what's "left over" at the end of each month. The four people behind Coffee Catering all have other jobs, and they've decided to not take any money from the company until its net profits are over $1,000 a month. Partners keep track of how many hours they're working, though, and the operating agreement of the company says that after the company gets to $1,000 a month in net profit, each person will receive payment for the work they've done.

Coffee Catering makes an estimate of what their P&L will look like for each month of their first year of operations. This shows what they expect to make and spend over the next 12 months.

A P&L for a Company's First Year of Operations

(In the interest of space, this chart shows only the first three months of projections, but it gives you a good idea about how to make the forecast.)

Income Statement for Coffee Catering	Start Up December	Jan	Feb	Mar
Total Sales		$ 1,098.00	$ 1,350.00	$ 1,650.00
Food Sales		$ 415.00	$ 600.00	$ 750.00
Beverage Sales		$ 683.00	$ 750.00	$ 900.00
COGS (direct costs)		$ 591.10	$ 681.25	$ 778.75
Food materials		$ 103.75	$ 150.00	$ 187.50
Beverage materials		$ 102.45	$ 112.50	$ 135.00
Labor		$ -	$ -	$ -
Rent		$ 100.00	$ 100.00	$ 100.00
Insurance		$ 50.00	$ 50.00	$ 50.00
Supplies		$ 80.00	$ 101.25	$ 123.75
Truck rental		$ 100.00	$ 100.00	$ 100.00
Gas		$ 54.90	$ 67.50	$ 82.50
Gross Profit		$ 506.90	$ 668.75	$ 871.25
SG&A		$ 140.00	$ 140.00	$ 140.00
Marketing		$ 75.00	$ 75.00	$ 75.00
Sales expenses		$ 40.00	$ 40.00	$ 40.00
Depreciation		$ 25.00	$ 25.00	$ 25.00
Operating Profit		$ 366.90	$ 528.75	$ 731.25
Interest Income and other		$ 4.10	$ 4.70	$ 5.67
Interest Expense and other		$ 16.67	$ 16.39	$ 16.11
Loan repayment, principal		$ 33.33	$ 33.61	$ 33.89
Interest Expense and other		$ 16.67	$ 16.39	$ 16.11
Earnings before taxes		$ 354.33	$ 517.06	$ 720.81
Taxes (30% est)		$ 106.30	$ 155.12	$ 216.24
Net Profit/(Loss)		$ 248.03	$ 361.94	$ 504.57

Imagine a business as a bathtub, with sales being water coming into the tub from the faucet, and costs being water going down the drain. The P&L shows the flows of your business: it tracks what's coming in and going out.

The next item we'll look at is the balance sheet, which measures the stock, or level, of the tub at a particular point in time. The P&L, then, is like a live-action video, since it's showing something that's in motion—water's coming in and water's going out; the balance sheet is like a still photo of the tub, showing you how much water is in it at the time the picture was taken.

The Balance Sheet

The balance sheet, or B/S, shows what you own and what you owe at the beginning and end of each time period. Coffee Catering's B/S starts even before their business does; their B/S begins on December, and they update it at the end of each month.

It's easy to understand why a P&L has that name -- it shows a company's profit or loss each month. How did the balance sheet get its name?

The balance sheet is called that because there are essentially two parts to it: What you own (your assets) and what you owe (your liabilities). The two sides always balance out.

Let's look at Coffee Catering's beginning B/S for December.

The company's assets are cash, inventories (supplies of food, beverages, paper plates and cups, etc.), and PP&E (or Property, Plant, and Equipment -- this can be real estate the company owns, machinery used to manufacture a product, or other equipment necessary to the business; in Coffee Catering's case, the PP&E are coffee makers and some catering equipment). The total value of the company's assets is $3,000.

When Coffee Catering is starting up, the company has two liabilities: $150 in "deferred compensation" and a $2,000 loan from the bank.

The deferred compensation is money that the partners "owe themselves" for work they've done for the business. If one of the partners has spent 15 hours working for the company before the business had started—buying supplies, making plans, marketing to potential customers, and doing other work—and it's agreed that partners will earn $10/hour for work done for the firm, then Coffee Catering owes him or her $150. Since the company doesn't want to use its cash to pay partners before the business gets to profitability, they decide to "defer" this compensation. Once profits hit $1,000/month, the company will start paying partners back— perhaps with interest—for the work they've done for the company.

If you take the company's assets of $3,000 and subtract the $2,150 of liabilities, there's $850 "left over." This is known as Shareholder's Equity (S/E), or net worth. Shareholder's equity can be thought of as what the company "owes" the owners (it shows up in the same side of the balance sheet as the liabilities). Assets are shown on the left side of the B/S, and liabilities and S/E are shown on the right side. You'll see that the left side of the B/S always balances with the right side. If it doesn't, there's an error in the B/S.

Assets and liabilities are usually divided into two categories: short-term and long-term. Typically, short-term assets are those that you expect to use in the next twelve months, while short-term liabilities are those that are due in the next year. Long-term assets and liabilities are those that aren't expected to be used or come due in the next twelve months.

Coffee Catering's initial balance sheet looks like this:

The Balance Sheet for Coffee Catering

Assets			Liabilities & Shareholder's Equity		
Current Assets:			**Current Liabilities:**		
Cash and cash equivalents	$	1,640.00	Short-term borrowings	$	-
Short-term investments	$	-	Accounts payable	$	-
Accounts receivable	$	-	Accrued taxes	$	-
Inventories	$	360.00	Current portion of LTD	$	-
Prepaid expenses and other	$	-	Accrued compensation	$	150.00
Total Current Assets	**$**	**2,000.00**	**Total Current Liabilities**	**$**	**150.00**
Long-Term Assets:			**Long-Term Liabilities:**		
PP&E, net	$	1,000.00	Bank debt	$	2,000.00
Other LT Assets	$	-	**Total LT Liabilities**	**$**	**2,000.00**
Total Long-Term Assets	**$**	**1,000.00**	**Total Liabilities**	**$**	**2,150.00**
			Total Shareholder's Equity	**$**	**850.00**
Total Assets	**$**	**3,000.00**	**Total Liabilities and S/E**	**$**	**3,000.00**

Once business starts in January, the Balance Sheet will change: inventories might rise or fall, the company might use some of its profits to pay off part of the bank debt, and it's possible that the business will have some accounts payables or accounts receivables. (Accounts payables are liabilities—they're money you owe to someone, like a supplier, but haven't paid yet; accounts receivables are assets—money that you're owed by someone.)

Each month, Coffee Catering will make updates to its balance sheet. For their planning purposes, though, they're going to make 12 months' worth of balance sheet forecasts.

Cash Flow Statements

The Cash Flow Statement, or CF, is the third and final type of financial statement we'll look at. As the name implies, CF statements show the flow of cash in and out of a business. You might be thinking that sounds a lot like what the P&L shows, but there are a few key differences.

One difference is what is known as a "non-cash charge." Non-cash charges are those that you count as a cost on your P&L, but which don't actually have any cash flow associated with them. Depreciation is one of the most common examples of a non-cash charge.

Most equipment depreciates over time. That means that the value of the equipment is worth less when it's a year old than when it's new. When it's two years old, it's worth even less.

Even if you've never heard the term "depreciation," if you've ever owned or thought about buying a car you're probably very familiar with the concept. It's said that the value of a new car falls 20 percent as soon as you drive it off the lot. As soon as you leave the dealership, it's no longer a new car, it's a used one, and a $25,000 car will fall to $20,000 in value when it's used (at least according to this rule of thumb). Each year, as you use the car, the value will decline. If you try to sell it when it's five years old, with 60,000 miles on it, the value of the car might be only $10,000. In that case, the value of the car has depreciated by $10,000 over the five years you've owned it (an average of $2,000 per year).

Suppose that Coffee Catering buys some equipment necessary to run their business. The equipment costs $1,000 and is expected to last for 40 months, at which time the value will have fallen to zero. The depreciation, then, would be $25/month for 40 months. When the company buys the equipment, $1,000 comes out of the cash on their balance sheet and their PP&E increases by $1,000. (Note that, overall, there's not a net change to the balance sheet; assets are just shifted from one area – cash -- to another --PP&E. Cash goes down by $1,000, and PPE goes up the same amount, so total assets don't change when the equipment is purchased.) As the equipment is used, though, the value falls by $25/month, so after a month of use, their PP&E balance is reduced to $975.

Coffee Catering considers depreciation an indirect cost for their business—an SG&A item. If the company does $1,000 of business in one month and had no other cost besides depreciation, their operating profit would be the $1,000 of revenue minus the monthly depreciation amount of $25, or $975.

Notice that depreciation isn't a cash charge: you don't pay cash for it the way you pay cash for coffee beans, catering supplies, or rent. Rather, depreciation is a non-cash charge, something that you have to account for, but which doesn't take cash out of your pocket. Your equipment might be losing $25/month in value, but you're not taking cash out of your wallet or bank account to pay that $25 expense each month.

The CF statement is different from the P&L in that it looks only at changes to cash, not changes to asset values. Let's look at Coffee Catering's cash flow statement for the month of December, when they expect to register their business.

Coffee Catering's Cash Flow Statement for December

Total Operating Cash Flow		
Investing Cash Flow:		
Purchase of Inventory & Supplies	$	(360.00)
Purchase of Equipment	$	(1,000.00)
Other		
Total Investing Cash Flow	**$**	**(1,360.00)**
Financing Cash Flow:		
Increase in LT Loan	$	2,000.00
Decreast in LT Loan		
Other	$	1,000.00
Total Financing Cash Flow	**$**	**3,000.00**
Total Cash Flow	**$**	**1,640.00**
Cash at beginning of period	$	-
Cash at end of period	$	1,640.00

First, notice that the company splits its cash flows into three different types: Operating Cash Flow, Investing Cash Flow, and Financing Cash Flow.

Operating Cash Flow is the cash flow directly tied to the company's business (it's "operations"): If the company has a net profit, it will show up in this portion of the monthly cash flow. If there's a change in inventory, it will show up here, as the inventory is used up or added to as the company conducts its business.

This is also where depreciation is "added back" to the company's net profit: because we took depreciation out of the P&L when calculating the company's net profit, we have to add it back in the cash flow statement since there was never any cash actually spent on it.

Since the company hasn't started operations yet, there are no operating cash flows. When business starts in January, we'll see flows in this section of the statement.

Investing cash flow is money that is invested in the company, or taken out of the company's investments. Buying new equipment or supplies would be considered an investment in the company, so those things would show up in this section of the cash flow statement. In December, the month before their business starts operations, the kids at Coffee Catering invest $1,360 in the company: $360 for inventory and supplies (these would be perishable items like coffee beans, cream and sweetener, paper cups, and so on) and $1,000 for equipment (durable equipment such as coffee makers and catering equipment).

Financing cash flow shows money that is raised through financing activities, such as money received through a bank loan or money contributed by the founders of the business or from investors. Coffee Catering received a $2,000 bank loan (due in five years, so it's called a Long-Term, or "LT" Loan). The founders also put in $1,000 of their own money to start the business, which they classify as "Other" financing cash flow.

You can see that the total cash flow for the month of December is $1,640: $3,000 raised for the business from the owners' investment and a bank loan, less the $1,360 worth of investment in equipment and supplies.

Finally, at the very bottom of the cash flow statement, you can see the beginning cash balance and the ending cash balance. Coffee Catering didn't have anything at the beginning of December, so the beginning cash balance is zero; at the end of the month – after all the cash flow activities -- the cash balance was $1,640.

Connecting All the Financial Statements

The beauty of the financial statements we're looking at is that they each perform an important and specific function, but they each are linked to one another. The net profit from Coffee Catering's P&L will show up in the company's operating cash flows; the cash on the balance sheet at the beginning of each month will show up at the bottom of the cash flow statement, and the change in cash flow for the month will result in an ending cash balance that will match the cash amount on the balance sheet at the end of the month. So the big thee financial statements all flow into one another.

When it's all done, this is what a set of financial statements—the P&L, cash flow, and B/S—for Coffee Catering looks like:

A Complete Set of Financials for Coffee Catering's First Three Months of Operations

(To conserve space, these financials only cover the first three months of the Company's financials.)

Income Statement for Coffee Catering	Start Up December	Jan	Feb	Mar
Total Sales	$	$ 1,098.00	$ 1,350.00	$ 1,650.00
Food Sales	$	$ 415.00	$ 600.00	$ 750.00
Beverage Sales	$	$ 683.00	$ 750.00	$ 900.00
COGS (direct costs)	$	$ 591.10	$ 681.25	$ 778.75
Food materials	$	$ 103.75	$ 150.00	$ 187.50
Beverage materials	$	$ 102.45	$ 112.50	$ 135.00
Labor	$	$ -	$ -	$ -
Rent	$	$ 100.00	$ 100.00	$ 100.00
Insurance	$	$ 50.00	$ 50.00	$ 50.00
Supplies	$	$ 80.00	$ 101.25	$ 123.75
Truck rental	$	$ 100.00	$ 100.00	$ 100.00
Gas	$	$ 54.90	$ 67.50	$ 82.50
Gross Profit	$	$ 506.90	$ 668.75	$ 871.25
SG&A	$	$ 140.00	$ 140.00	$ 140.00
Marketing	$	$ 75.00	$ 75.00	$ 75.00
Sales expenses	$	$ 40.00	$ 40.00	$ 40.00
Depreciation	$	$ 25.00	$ 25.00	$ 25.00
Operating Profit	$	$ 366.90	$ 528.75	$ 731.25
Interest Income and other	$	$ 4.10	$ 4.70	$ 5.67
Interest Expense and other	$	$ 16.67	$ 16.39	$ 16.11
Loan repayment, principal	$	$ 33.33	$ 33.61	$ 33.89
Interest Expense and other	$	$ 16.67	$ 16.39	$ 16.11
Earnings before taxes	$	$ 354.33	$ 517.06	$ 720.81
Taxes (30% est.)	$	$ 106.30	$ 155.12	$ 216.24
Net Profit/(Loss)	$	$ 248.03	$ 361.94	$ 504.57

Cash Flow Statement for Coffee Catering	December		Jan		Feb		Mar	
Operating Cash Flow:								
Net Earnings after Tax			$	248.03	$	361.94	$	504.57
Depreciation			$	25.00	$	25.00	$	25.00
Change in Accounts Receivable			$	-	$	-	$	-
Change in Inventory			$	286.20	$	363.75	$	446.25
Change in Accounts Payable			$	-	$	-	$	-
Total Operating Cash Flow			**$**	**559.23**	**$**	**750.69**	**$**	**975.82**
Investing Cash Flow:								
Purchase of Inventory & Supplies	$	(360.00)	$	(286.20)	$	(363.75)	$	(446.25)
Purchase of Equipment	$	(1,000.00)						
Other			$	-	$	-	$	-
Total Investing Cash Flow	**$**	**(1,360.00)**	**$**	**(286.20)**	**$**	**(363.75)**	**$**	**(446.25)**
Financing Cash Flow:								
Increase in LT Loan	$	2,000.00	$	-	$	-	$	-
Decreast in LT Loan			$	(33.33)	$	(33.61)	$	(33.89)
Other	$	1,000.00	$	-	$	-	$	-
Total Financing Cash Flow	**$**	**3,000.00**	**$**	**(33.33)**	**$**	**-**	**$**	**-**
Total Cash Flow	**$**	**1,640.00**	**$**	**239.70**	**$**	**386.94**	**$**	**529.57**
Cash at beginning of period	$	-	$	1,640.00	$	1,879.70	$	2,266.64
Cash at end of period	$	1,640.00	$	1,879.70	$	2,266.64	$	2,796.21

Balance Sheet					
Current Assets:		**Dec**	**Jan**	**Feb**	**Mar**
Cash and cash equivalents	$	1,640.00	$ 1,879.70	$ 2,266.64	$ 2,796.21
Short-term investments	$	-			
Accounts receivable	$	-			
Inventories	$	360.00	$ 360.00	$ 360.00	$ 360.00
Prepaid expenses and other					
Total Current Assets	**$**	**2,000.00**	**$ 2,239.70**	**$ 2,626.64**	**$ 3,156.21**
Long-Term Assets:					
PP&E, net	$	1,000.00	$ 975.00	$ 950.00	$ 925.00
Other LT Assets	$	-			
Total Long-Term Assets	**$**	**1,000.00**	**$ 975.00**	**$ 950.00**	**$ 925.00**
Total Assets	**$**	**3,000.00**	**$ 3,214.70**	**$ 3,576.64**	**$ 4,081.21**
Current Liabilities:					
Short-term borrowings	$	-			
Accounts payable	$	-			
Accrued taxes	$	-			
Accrued compensation	$	150.00	$ 274.50	$ 337.50	$ 412.50
Total Current Liabilities	**$**	**150.00**			
Long-Term Liabilities:					
Bank debt	$	2,000.00	$ 1,966.67	$ 1,933.06	$ 1,899.16
Total LT Liabilities	**$**	**2,000.00**	**$ 1,966.67**	**$ 1,933.06**	**$ 1,899.16**
Total Liabilities	**$**	**2,150.00**	**$ 2,241.17**	**$ 2,270.56**	**$ 2,311.66**
Total Shareholder's Equity	**$**	**850.00**	**$ 973.53**	**$ 1,306.09**	**$ 1,769.54**

Why Is This So Hard!?!

Okay, I know this looks intimidating to someone who's never seen it before. There are a lot of numbers, and a lot of areas that connect with others. It looks like an impossible puzzle. I have four pieces of advice that can help make this easier:

1. Take things one small step at a time.
2. Realize that while the whole puzzle might look large and intimidating, the pieces are easy to connect to one another.
3. Don't worry if you don't get it all right the first time.
4. Don't be afraid to ask for help.

When you're walking a tightrope across a canyon, don't look down. Similarly, when you're starting out on making your first set of financial statements, don't look at the whole, long, complicated set of documents staring you in the face—you might freeze up. On the tightrope, you'd look straight ahead, concentrating on slowly moving one foot in front of the other, inching your way across the canyon you're trying to cross. If you apply the same strategy to your financial statements, not thinking about the entire task, but focusing on getting through each piece, you'll find that you can cover a lot of ground.

While a P&L or cash flow statement might seem like a nightmare of complexity, the individual pieces aren't so difficult, and you'll see that the basic building blocks of business are very simple and apply almost universally.

Lets' try to make things a little easier by breaking the components of the financial statements down into easily-manageable pieces: Start with forecasting your sales. What are you going to sell? How much do you think you can make?

Every company in the world follows a simple formula when it comes to sales: how many units they expect to sell and how much they will charge per unit. If you're in the babysitting business, you might expect to sell ten "units" (a unit in this case would be an hour of your time) at $10 each, generating sales of $100; a coffee shop might sell 100 cups of coffee at $2 each, meaning that total sales are $200.

Total Units x Unit Price = Total Sales. It doesn't get much simpler than that.

Next, Sales - Costs = Profits. Every business in the world, from nonprofit charities to mega-conglomerates, lives by this simple formula.

Where do the profits go? If they go into your company's checking account, you'll see that on the balance sheet. The cash on your balance sheet will match up with the cash on your cash flow statement.

Finally, don't get too stressed out about the financial forecasts. If you work on them for a while and keep getting stuck, move on. Move on to working on other parts of the business and stop thinking about the financials for a while. Come back to them later, when you're fresh and able to look at them again without tearing your hair out.

If you give it your best shot and still can't get comfortable with making financial statements for your business, you should look for some help. An accountant or someone with a strong financial background will be able to help you with these; hopefully, they'll appreciate your ambition and give you some free advice, but even if you have to pay a professional for showing you how to put the financials together, the cost of doing that will be small compared to what you stand to lose if you don't have a good set of financials.

You can pay someone to make your financials for you, but you probably shouldn't do that. If you ever talk to a potential investor or lender, they'll want to go through your financials in great detail, and they'll expect you to answer a lot of questions about them. If you've gone through the work of making them, you'll know them backward and forward; if you've outsourced the job, it will be clear to everyone that you don't know anything about the numbers they're looking at, and it's unlikely they'll give you their money.

How to Use the Financial Statements for Business Analysis

Putting the figures into your financial statements is a very important part of business planning, but basically it's just data entry. Data are only useful when you know how to analyze them, and that's what we will look at in this section.

The Break-Even Analysis

One important type of financial study is the Break-Even, or B-E, analysis. The B-E analysis will show you how many units of your product you will need to sell to cover all of your costs. You might be surprised at how many businesspeople couldn't tell you how many pieces of equipment their company has to sell or how many hours of work they have to do in order to cover all their company's expenses.

There are four things you need to know in order to do a B-E analysis:

Step 1. You need to know what your "average revenue per unit" is.

This can also be called "the average transaction amount". For instance, if Coffee Catering has $1,098 worth of sales per month, selling drinks or food to 200 customers, then their average revenue per unit is $5.49. (Technically, there are important differences between average revenues per unit and average transaction amounts, but I'm trying to keep things simple, so we'll use the terms interchangeably.)

Doing a Break-Even Analysis, Part 1: Average Revenue per Unit

Average Revenue for Coffee Catering (Revenue per Unit)		
Average Food Sale per Customer	$	3.74
Average Beverage Sale per Customer	$	1.75
Total Average Sale per Customer	**$**	**5.49**

Step 2: You need to know what your fixed costs (FC) are.

A fixed cost is one that doesn't change based on the amount of business you do. Rent, insurance, and equipment rentals are all fixed costs: the amount a store pays in rent doesn't vary based on how many customers come in during a given month; and the amount a company has to pay for a monthly truck rental usually isn't based on how many times they use it.

Step 3: You need to know what your variable costs (VC) are.

Variable costs are those that fluctuate based on the units your company sells. If you sell cupcakes, then flour and sugar would be variable costs: If you sell 1,000 cupcakes, you'll spend a lot more on these ingredients than if you sell only 10. If you're in the business of tutoring kids, you might have only one variable cost, the cost of the gas you need to drive to and from your customers' homes.

Look at the January P&L for Coffee Catering, and try to classify the company's costs as either fixed or variable (you'll see the answers in a moment).

Doing a Break-Even Analysis, Part 2: Identifying Variable Costs

Income Statement for Coffee Catering		Jan	
Total Sales	$	1,098.00	
Food Sales	$	415.00	
Beverage Sales	$	683.00	Fixed or Variable?
COGS (direct costs)	$	591.10	
Food materials	$	103.75	
Beverage materials	$	102.45	
Labor	$	-	
Rent	$	100.00	
Insurance	$	50.00	
Supplies	$	80.00	
Truck rental	$	100.00	
Gas	$	54.90	
Gross Profit	$	506.90	Fixed or Variable?
SG&A	$	140.00	
Marketing	$	75.00	
Sales expenses	$	40.00	
Depreciation	$	25.00	
Operating Profit	$	366.90	
Interest Income and other	$	4.10	
Interest Expense and other	$	16.67	
Loan repayment, principal	$	33.33	
Interest Expense and other	$	16.67	
Earnings before taxes	$	354.33	
Taxes (30% est.)	$	106.30	
Net Profit/(Loss)	$	248.03	

For Coffee Catering, the fixed costs are as follows:

Doing a Break-Even Analysis, Part 3: Identifying Fixed Costs

Total Fixed Costs:		
Rent	$	100.00
Insurance	$	50.00
Truck rental	$	100.00
Depreciation	$	25.00
Marketing	$	75.00
Sales expenses	$	40.00
Total FC	$	390.00

Step 4: You need to know what the variable costs per unit of sales are.

Take the total variable cost and divide it by the number of sales units. The total variable costs are simply the company's total costs minus its fixed costs. For Coffee Catering, the total variable costs are $341.10.

Doing a Break-Even Analysis, Part 4: Finding Variable Costs per Unit of Sales

Total Variable Costs	
Food materials	$ 103.75
Beverage materials	$ 102.45
Labor	$ -
Supplies	$ 80.00
Gas	$ 54.90
Total FC	**$ 341.10**

We know that the company had 200 units of sales (or 200 transactions), so the average variable cost per unit is $1.71.

You now have all the pieces necessary to do a B-E analysis.

Take the average revenue per unit and subtract the variable cost per unit from it. For Coffee Catering, the average sale is $5.49, and the variable cost per sale is $1.71. The gross profit per sale, then, is $3.78.

Finally, take your total fixed costs and divide that amount by the gross profit per sale, and that will show you how many units you need to sell in order to break even. In Coffee Catering's case, they must have 103 (well, 103.2, but we'll round it down a bit) transactions per month at $5.49 per transaction in order to break even.

How much profit will Coffee Catering make if they sold 10 units more than their B-E level (in other words, what would their profit be if they had 113 sales, rather than 103)? Once you've done the B-E analysis, it's easy to figure out the answer: If the company sells 10 units more than they need to break even, and each unit has a gross profit of $3.78, then their total profit would be $37.80 -- remember, we don't have to consider the fixed costs any longer, since the first 103 units covered them all, so every sale after the 103rd one is profitable.

Break-Even Analysis		
Avg. Sale Amount	$	5.49
Less variable cost	$	(1.71)
Gross Profit/Sale	$	3.78
Total Fixed Cost	$	390.00
# of Sales to cover FC		103.2

The Source and Use of Funds Statement

If you go into a bank asking for a loan to start up your business, one thing the bank is going to want to know is "What are you going to use the money for?" The source and use of funds statement shows people involved with your business how much money you need, how it's going to be spent, and where that money is expected to come from.

If you've made a balance sheet for your company, then making a source and use of funds statement becomes very easy to do.

We know from Coffee Catering's initial balance sheet that they expect to raise $3,000 in funds: $2,000 from a bank loan and $1,000 from "owner contributions," or money the partners put into the business to help start it up. We see that $1,000 of their capital will go for the purchase of equipment and $360 for the purchase of disposable supplies. They'll keep $1,640 in cash in the bank, which we'll call "working capital." Working capital is the term used for money set aside for near-term business use—for buying new supplies, paying utility bills, or making other payments that are required to operate the business before it starts generating enough cash flow to cover these payments.

Here's what Coffee Catering's start-up balance sheet looks like:

A Company's Balance Sheet at Start-Up

Current Assets:			Current Liabilities:		
Cash and cash equivalents	$	1,640.00	Short-term borrowings	$	-
Short-term investments	$	-	Accounts payable	$	-
Accounts receivable	$	-	Accrued taxes	$	-
Inventories	$	360.00	Current portion of LTD	$	-
Prepaid expenses and other	$	-	Accrued compensation	$	150.00
Total Current Assets	**$**	**2,000.00**	**Total Current Liabilities**	**$**	**150.00**
Long-Term Assets:			Long-Term Liabilities:		
PP&E, net	$	1,000.00	Bank debt	$	2,000.00
Other LT Assets	$	-	**Total LT Liabilities**	**$**	**2,000.00**
Total Long-Term Assets	**$**	**1,000.00**	**Total Liabilities**	**$**	**2,150.00**
			Total Shareholder's Equity	**$**	**850.00**
Total Assets	**$**	**3,000.00**	**Total Liabilities and S/E**	**$**	**3,000.00**

From this, we can create the following source and use of funds statement:

Source and Use of Funds Statement

Coffee Catering Source and Use of Funds Statement				
Source of Funds	**Amount**		**Use of Funds**	**Amount**
Bank Loan	$	2,000.00	Purchase of Equipment	$ 1,000.00
Owner Investment	$	1,000.00	Purchase of Supplies	$ 360.00
			Working Capital	$ 1,640.00
Total Sources	**$**	**3,000.00**	**Total Uses**	**$ 3,000.00**

The source and use of funds statement is usually only necessary when you're raising capital. You don't need to make or update this document regularly, only when you plan to ask a bank or investor for money to put into your business.

(A more advanced, but logical question, is "how much working capital do I need?" Working capital is the money that you need to operate your business from the time you have bills to the time you receive payments from customers to cover the bills – it's "tide us over" money. I won't go through a complicated analysis of how to determine exactly how much working capital you need; I just don't want you to get the impression that every dollar that's "left over" between your source of funds and what you need automatically falls into the "working capital" category.)

The Financial Summary

Coffee Catering puts together a simple table showing their financial projections for a few key areas, as follows:

Coffee Catering's 5-Year Financial Forecast:

End of Calendar Year	Year 1	Year 2	Year 3	Year 4	Year 5
Sales	$ 28,548.00	$ 35,000.00	$ 45,000.00	$ 55,000.00	$ 70,000.00
Operating Profit	$ 13,998.15	$ 17,500.00	$ 22,000.00	$ 27,000.00	$ 34,000.00
Net Income	$ 9,403.43	$ 11,750.00	$ 14,700.00	$ 18,400.00	$ 23,000.00
Cash Flow	$ 7,070.10	$ 8,800.00	$ 11,000.00	$ 13,800.00	$ 17,250.00
Assets	$ 21,170.10	$ 26,500.00	$ 33,000.00	$ 41,500.00	$ 51,700.00
Shareholder's Equity	$ 8,816.06	$ 11,000.00	$ 13,800.00	$ 17,200.00	$ 21,500.00

The value of a start-up company making projections five years into the future is debatable. I think there's value in the exercise, but the reality is that very few people will believe that you can forecast sales and profits (much less other things) for your company five years into the future. We'll discuss this in more detail later.

If you do make longer-term financial projections for your company, you should be able to justify the assumptions. The summary table will show key items of sales, profits, and assets that will give the reader of your business plan a simple view of how much money you think you can make, but you'll need to explain the details – such as the number of units you expect to sell and the selling price, the different cost items and other figures behind those numbers.

Part 7: Other Types of Financial Statements

There are a couple of other types of financial statements that you should know about. You don't have to make them, but they aren't difficult to create if you have your basic set of statements done.

Common Size Statements

The first supplemental statement you could consider making is known as the "common size" statement. This statement is usually used for the P&L (though it can be applied to any financial statement). When it's used for the P&L, it usually shows what percentage of revenue the different P&L items are.

For example, Coffee Catering's common size income statement would look like this:

A Common-Size Income Statement

Common Size Income Statement for Coffee Catering	Start Up Dec	Jan	Feb	Mar
Total Sales		**100%**	**100%**	**100%**
Food Sales		38%	44%	45%
Beverage Sales		62%	56%	55%
COGS (direct costs)		**54%**	**50%**	**47%**
Food materials		9%	11%	11%
Beverage materials		9%	8%	8%
Labor		0%	0%	0%
Rent		9%	7%	6%
Insurance		5%	4%	3%
Supplies		7%	8%	8%
Truck rental		9%	7%	6%
Gas		5%	5%	5%
Gross Profit		**46%**	**50%**	**53%**
SG&A		**13%**	**10%**	**8%**
Marketing		7%	6%	5%
Sales expenses		4%	3%	2%
Depreciation		2%	2%	2%
Operating Profit		**33%**	**39%**	**44%**
Interest Income and other		0%	0%	0%
Interest Expense and other		2%	1%	1%
Loan repayment, principal		3%	2%	2%
Interest Expense and other		2%	1%	1%
Earnings before taxes		**32%**	**38%**	**44%**
Taxes (30% est.)		10%	11%	13%
Net Profit/(Loss)		**23%**	**27%**	**31%**

Notice that everything is expressed as a percentage of total revenues for each month.

This type of statement is useful to understand things like profit margins and to see exactly how big particular costs are relative to the company's sales.

Growth Statement

The growth statement is similar to the common size one in that it expresses everything in percentage terms. As its name implies, though, this statement shows growth rates for a company.

Coffee Catering's growth statement for its P&L would look like the following. The figures you see in February show the rate of growth compared to January, so a figure of 10 percent for "beverage materials" means that the company spent 10 percent more for beverage materials in February than it did in January. Each figure you see shows an item's rate of growth from the previous month.

A Growth Statement:

Growth Income Statement for Coffee Catering	Start Up Dec	Jan	Feb	Mar
Total Sales			**23%**	**22%**
Food Sales			45%	25%
Beverage Sales			10%	20%
COGS (direct costs)			**15%**	**14%**
Food materials			45%	25%
Beverage materials			10%	20%
Labor			0%	0%
Rent			0%	0%
Insurance			0%	0%
Supplies			27%	22%
Truck rental			0%	0%
Gas			23%	22%
Gross Profit			**32%**	**30%**
SG&A			**0%**	**0%**
Marketing			0%	0%
Sales expenses			0%	0%
Depreciation			0%	0%
Operating Profit			**44%**	**38%**
Interest Income and other			15%	21%
Interest Expense and other			-2%	-2%
Loan repayment, principal			1%	1%
Interest Expense and other			-2%	-2%
Earnings before taxes			**46%**	**39%**
Taxes (30% est.)			46%	39%
Net Profit/(Loss)			**46%**	**39%**

Another example: The company started in January. In February, its food sales grew 45% from the January levels. In March, food sales rose 25% from February levels.

Part 8: Do I Really Need to Do All This Extra Work?

I know all of this looks like it is very complicated and might take hundreds of hours, but the reality is that if you're familiar with Excel or any other type of spreadsheet software, you can make common size and growth statements in just a few minutes once your basic financial statements are done.

You'll spend a lot of time creating the basic financial statements — the income statement, balance sheet, and cash flow statement — but adding a source and use of funds statement, a common size statement, and a growth statement to your initial set of financial documents really won't add a lot of work to the process.

THE BASICS OF FINANCIAL ANALYSIS—WHAT TO LOOK FOR

These financial statements will allow you to identify key problem areas with your business at a glance. How can you do that? Look for what's changing and what's big.

What's Changing?

If you notice from your growth statement that something is changing at a high rate, it signals something you need to be aware of. If your labor costs are growing much faster than your sales are, it might be a problem that could wipe out your business if it's not addressed.

In Coffee Catering's case, labor costs were flat (growing at zero) for most of the year, and then really shot up. We know the reason for this: the company was deferring compensation to its partners until the business hit $1,000 a month in profits; once that happened, it started paying its employees (the partners) back for the work they had done in the past.

Eventually, accrued compensation will be paid off and the labor costs should grow at a much lower rate.

What's Big?

You don't have to concern yourself with every detail and every penny of your business. You should focus your attention on the big items. What's considered "big" when it comes to your financials? Generally, anything that's over 10 percent of your revenues, or that could become 10 percent or more in the next 12 months.

For example, you might notice that some cost item of your business is growing at a very fast rate. If that item is only two percent of your revenues, though, it will be a long time before it becomes significant: a cost that's two percent of revenue, growing at twenty percent a month isn't as much of a concern as a cost that's twenty-five percent of revenue growing at ten percent a month.

Putting It All Together

If something is big and growing, it deserves your immediate attention; if it's big but not growing, it's probably not a big concern; if it's growing but not big, you can probably defer thinking about it until more pressing matters are taken care of.

If you notice erratic patterns in your common size and growth statements, you should try to understand what's causing the volatility. For example, your business might be very seasonal: A snowplowing business will see much more in sales and costs in the winter than in the spring and summer.

If there's no reason you can think of for the type of monthly volatility you see in your financial statements, you will need to dig in and do some real research to find out why customers flock to you one month and abandon you the next, or why costs skyrocket some months and fall off a cliff during others.

Part 10: Other Things to Include in Your Financial Statements and Analysis

Main Assumptions

You should include a page titled "main assumptions" and attach it to your financial statements. This page will outline the assumptions that your financial models are based on. For example, a company that planned to sell hot dogs and other food from a catering cart at local high school football games or other events might have a set of key assumptions like the following:

- Number of sporting events our company will be set up at each month: 10

- Average number of people attending each sporting event: 100

- Percentage of attendees that will buy something from us: 20 percent

- Average sale per customer: $5.00

From these assumptions, we can understand how the company's sales forecast is made: if they expect to sell at 10 events per month, with each event generating 20 customers (20 percent of the 100 people at each event) and each customer spending $5.00, then the company's total sales would be expected to be $1,000 ($5 x 20 customers x 10 events) per month.

The company above might also have to list assumptions about its major cost items: How much food would have to be thrown away because it didn't sell? How much will the company pay people to work the catering cart? Will the schools allow the company to sell food at events, or will the company have to pay the school to operate at its events?

You can look at your list of business risks for other ideas of key assumptions you should outline. For example, if you have a "babysitting dispatch" service that takes $3 an hour for every babysitter you match up with a customer, a key risk might be getting a large enough pool of reliable and responsible baby-sitters for each Friday and Saturday night. You can outline your assumptions like this: "Our company's sales forecasts are based on the assumption that there will be ten sitters available each Friday and Saturday, that each sitter will be paid $10 an hour from the company, and that each sitting job lasts an average of three hours."

Long-Term Forecasts

Normally, I would advise that you include monthly forecasts for the first year of your business, and perhaps quarterly or semi-annual forecasts for the next two years. The reality is that most start-up businesses see so much change in their first twelve months that most of the long-term forecasts are rendered mean-ingless pretty quickly, so it's much more important that you spend your time getting things right on the short-term (6- or 12-month) forecasts, rather than spending much time on the long-term ones.

For a young person starting his or her own business, there's no need at all to make a forecast beyond the first year or so; making a truly long-term forecast (a forecast that tries to project business conditions four, five, or more years into the future) is a waste of time. Spend 95 percent of your time on the forecasts for the first twelve months of the business, and five percent of your time on Year Two. Don't worry about forecasting more than two years out unless you're expecting to run your business full-time (not as an after-school job or hobby), seek significant out-side funding, and really believe that you'll be in this business for the next five or more years. If these conditions apply, then you can make forecasts for the five-year period.

Sanity Check

A sanity check is simply a quick and dirty analysis of your financials to see if they make sense. What does that mean? It means stepping back from your financials, working in reverse, and seeing what the implications of your forecasts are.

Let me show you what I mean.

Suppose you want to start a business mowing lawns. You're going to do this with two friends and will try to get a bank loan for a truck to use in the business, so you've decided you need a business plan with a good set of financials. You make your financial forecast, which shows that you expect to be making $15,000 of revenues a month one year after launching. After subtracting all the costs of the business, you figure your company will have $5,000 a month in profits, even after paying each of the partners $10 an hour for their work. Looks great, right?

Now, step back from the forecast and reverse engineer your revenues: Dissect that $15,000 a month figure that you've forecasted for Month 12. If it's just the three of you working, that means that each of you would have to be generating $5,000 a month of revenue by then. Suppose each of you worked every single day of the month, or 30 days. If you did this, you'd each have to make about $170 a day to hit your numbers. Okay, how much will each job pay on average? Let's assume you calculated this to be $20 for one and a half hours of work. Based on your estimate of average revenue per unit, each of you would have to do eight jobs a day.

Now that you've stepped back and worked things in reverse, from the ending revenue figure all the way back to how much each of you will make on an average job, you can ask yourself, "Is the figure we're ending up with possible?"

It might be possible, but it sure doesn't seem likely. In order to make $15,000 of revenue with three people, your sanity check shows you'd have to do eight jobs a day (working 12 hours a day), seven days a week, for a month. And that doesn't even include the time it takes to drive between jobs, eat lunch, take breaks, and so on.

Sanity checks are how you can stop yourself from making basic financial mistakes. Some people just put simple formulas into their forecasts. They might assume, for example, that their sales will grow at 10 percent each month and that costs will rise at 5 percent a month. The problem is that this formula, if taken out long enough, would result in your company being the largest company the world's ever seen. If your company started with $1,000 in revenues and $750 of costs, and you grew those at 10 percent and 5 percent, respectively, each month, then in 20 years your monthly profits would be $7.8 trillion dollars a month— this is about what the entire countries of China and Germany produce in an entire year *combined*. A simple sanity check can let you know that forecasts that seem reasonable at first glance would lead to insane results if stretched out over time.

Part 11: Last Pieces of Advice About Your Financial Statements

1. Check your statements for consistency. Make sure that your balance sheet actually balances, and that the numbers in your cash flow statement are consistent with those in your income statement (P&L). Remember, the three key financial statements are linked to one another; check the links and make sure your data are correct.
2. Balance your ambition with a healthy dose of reality.

Remember, optimism is a great asset for an entrepreneur, but make sure your enthusiasm for your business doesn't lead to financial forecasts that aren't credible.

Part 12: What to Do with Your Financials When You're Done with Them

If you put the work into your financials, you'll end up with an important set of documents that you'll be able to comfortably and confidently go through in any level of detail with anyone. You will be proud of yourself, and you should be. Once you've created your first set of financial statements, the second set will be much, much easier to make. When you go back to your statements to update them, the process will be painless, and you'll be able to competently go through any other company's financials, knowing what to look for and being able to identify problems and opportunities.

The bad news is that although you've just scaled a very tall mountain and will want to shout with pride from the top, you have to bury all your work in the appendixes of your business plan. You might include some financial highlights in the main body of your business plan, but the guts of the statements will be attached, like an afterthought, to the back of your document.

Don't fret, though: Most sophisticated businesspeople who look at your plan will view the non-financial stuff as mere appetizers before sinking their teeth into the financials at the back. The reason your financial statements are put at the back is that they require a shift in gears from the casual reading of narrative that makes up the body of a business plan. It would be awkward to have page after page of detailed financial models in the middle of a more fluid explanation of concepts and approaches; putting all your financials in the body of your business plan is like having to break into a 10-minute sprint in the middle of a leisurely hour-long jog.

Don't make the mistake of thinking that just because your financials are in the appendixes they're not important or that people won't look at them. Good financial statements are what separate the men from the boys (or the women from the girls, as the case may be). Many financial experts (such as bank loan officers or investors) will view most of the content of your business plan besides the financial statements as simply "fluff." Some might even skip the body of the business plan and jump directly to the financial models when looking at your business. Finance is a universal language, and the people who speak it well are able to find just about everything they need to know by looking through your financial statements.

Chapter 9:

The Funding Request

This section of the plan is where you identify your funding needs and ask for capital. Most small start-ups, particularly those created by young people, are started with personal savings and access to other personal funds (for example, selling an asset, such as a car or savings bond). Sometimes, though, "owner capital" is not enough to launch a business, and funding from external sources is needed. In this section, we'll look at the two approaches to funding a start-up: using one's own money and using OPM ("Other People's Money").

The first step of this process is understanding the financial needs of your business. Does your company need more money than you and your immediate circle (friends, partners, the Bank of Mom & Dad) can provide? The answer to this question should come out after you've made the financial models of the business.

If your financials show that you need $1,000 more than you have to launch the business, and $200 per month of additional funds to grow the business, you may decide to seek out a total of $3,500 in outside capital, to ensure you have enough to start the company and run it for awhile.

When you seek this capital out, whether it be from a traditional lender or from a potential investor (avenues we'll cover in detail later), it will be important for you to show that party at least two things: 1) the source and use of funds statement (covered in the financials section, and explaining how the money you're asking for will be used); and 2) what's in it for the person giving you money. (For a lender, it could be getting a good rate of interest on their loan and creating a banking relationship with what could be a very big and successful company in the future; for an investor, it could be the possibility of buying into the next Google, Starbucks, or Apple.)

Let's look at the benefits and risks of different avenues of funding for a start-up business.

Starting with Your Own Money

If you start out with your own capital, using money you've put away and saved or invested, you're likely to retain more control over your business and keep more of any profits it makes.

The main downside with self-funding your business is that if it fails, you could be left with nothing. Putting everything you have into a new business can create a lot of stress if things are slow to take off at work and you aren't able to pay rent or buy groceries.

One big thing you have going for you is your youth: If you start a business when you're very young, put everything you have into it, and then fail, you at least have the rest of your life to recoup your losses. Plus, you'll have earned an education in business that many people never have the opportunity to obtain.

When you begin taking money from other people, though, the dynamics of your company change completely. Generally, people who give you money for your business (if it's not a gift) are making an investment in your business. Just as you can invest your money in bonds or stocks, people or institutions can invest in you. You can sell part of your company to someone else— known as "equity financing," since you're raising capital by selling equity in your business—or you can finance your company with loans, which is referred to as "debt financing." Let's look at some of the dynamics of these methods.

Starting with OPM (Other People's Money): Debt Financing

You're probably familiar with the concept of debt on some level: A debt is something you owe someone else. If you borrow $20 from your mom, you are "indebted" to her, and need to pay her back. Your mom might even make you promise to pay it back within some fixed period of time and give her something on top of what she's lent you: "you can have the $20, but you have to clean your room first and promise to pay me back by next Friday." The amount of the loan a person gives you is called "principal," and what that person is getting "on top" of the principal is usually a fee or interest.

Banks, credit unions and other financial institutions have loan officers that people can speak with about personal or business loans. These bank officials will look at the loan request, consider the borrower's financial situation (credit score, employment, history with the financial institution, and other factors) and decide whether or not to grant the loan and what conditions to set for its repayment. For the lender (the bank), the money they give someone is a loan; for the borrower, the money they receive is a debt. If you borrow money from a bank (or even friends or family members), you have a debt to repay them.

Parts of a Loan

There are three main components to most loans from professional lenders: principal, interest, and fees. These are pretty straightforward.

A. **Principal** is the amount of money loaned to you, or the amount you owe at any given time. For example, if you borrow $1,000 to launch your business, the initial principal on the loan is $1,000. If, after six months of making payments, you still owe $500 on that loan, the $500 is your principal balance.

B. **Interest** is the amount you're being charged to use someone else's money. This amount is usually stated as a percentage, and can generally be either a "fixed rate" or a "floating rate." For example, a bank may lend you $1,000 on the condition that you repay the $1,000 principal with five percent interest (fixed) within one year. Alternatively, the interest rate might not be fixed at five percent, but could be based on some "benchmark rate" and formula, such as "prime + three percent," which means the prime interest rate (the rate at which banks lend money to their most trustworthy clients, and which can be found each day in most newspapers or financial websites) plus an additional three percent. If the current prime rate is three percent, then the interest rate the borrower needs to pay will be six percent; if prime rises to four percent, then the interest rate one pays will rise to seven percent.

C. **Fees** are charges you pay someone for setting up and/ or administering a loan. For example, a bank may loan you $1,000 on a one-year fixed 10 percent interest rate, but charge a "loan origination fee" of $50 up front and a "management fee" of $60 per year. So, if you borrow $1,000, you'll actually receive only $950, with $50 being used to pay the origination fee.

This discussion is intentionally simplistic. There are many other things that one should consider when borrowing money. For example, consider the compounding terms -- i.e., is the five percent interest charged once a year, or is that five percent charged every month? The answer can make a big difference in the amount you eventually repay. You will also need to know if there are any prepayment penalties, and to be sure you know the potential effects of the loan on your personal assets and credit (i.e., if you're putting up collateral for a loan and miss a payment, you could lose what you've pledged).

The loan officer at the bank you're dealing with will have to walk you through all the key points and terms of the loan. The best piece of advice I can give you when it comes to considering a loan from a financial institution is this: Don't be too shy or proud to ask questions -- a lot of people have gotten into trouble because they didn't understand the terms of a loan but were too embarrassed to ask for clarification on each point.

Lines of Credit

Another approach that many businesses take in accessing capital from banks and financial institutions is setting up a Line of Credit (LOC). A bank might give you an LOC of, say, $10,000 that you can tap into as needed from time to time, usually with no collateral required to gain approval. You'll still have a payback period and still have to pay interest on the money you use, but the LOC is different from a loan in that you only pay for what you use. In other words, if you take a loan for $10,000, you might not need all of that right away, but you're paying interest on the entire amount. With an LOC of $10,000, you could access up to $10,000, but if you start by taking out only $2,000, your interest payment is based only on that amount.

A business LOC is a very common form of financing offered by most banks. The amount of the LOC your business is able to get depends on things like your company's past revenues and projected cash flows. If you can show that you will have enough cash flow to cover debt payments each month, you may be able to receive an LOC from a bank. The LOC is similar to a credit card, in that the debt is "revolving"—typically, payment terms are based on adjustable interest rates, and you can elect to pay the entire balance at any time without penalties.

Other Sources of Debt Financing

There are many places to get loans from – banks, credit unions, and crowd funding sites are perhaps the most obvious, but there are also government and community organizations that offer loans to start-ups and small businesses. The Small Business Administration is one example of an organization that encourages and supports small businesses with loans and other resources (although the SBA doesn't lend directly to businesses, it can help companies get loans – see the sidebox for more information).

If you receive a loan from a friend or family member, my suggestion is that you treat the loan as a bank loan, even if the lender is much more casual with how they're willing to view the money they've given you. You could save yourself a lot of problems if you insist that a loan agreement be drafted up, showing the amount you're borrowing, what the payment terms are (how much in interest, when the loan will be due, and other points), and what would happen in the event of a default (if you're unable to pay back the loan). What happens if the friend who lent you the money believes that she's entitled to "call in" the loan at any time, whereas you believed you had six months to pay her back? A loan document is a contract that should set out certain important information for the lender and borrower to agree on before the loan is made.

Secured and Unsecured Loans

Typically, loans can be secured or unsecured. A "secured" loan is one that has some collateral behind it. A $3,000 loan might be "backed" by your $10,000 car, so the lender could take that collateral if you don't fulfill all of your loan-repayment responsibilities (even if you pay back $2,900 of that $3,000 loan, if you fail to make that last payment, you could lose your

$10,000 vehicle). An "unsecured" loan is one that doesn't have collateral behind it.

Many people make the mistake of thinking that banks make loans based on the collateral you have to offer them as protection for their loan, but that's not usually the case. Banks aren't in the business of repossessing cars and trucks and then trying to sell them, so they're less likely to make loans based on your collateral than they are on what they view as your "ability to pay."

To assess one's ability to repay a loan, a bank will look at your credit history and score, your banking relationship with them (i.e., whether you have been a good customer with them for years, or someone who's just walked in off the street asking for money), and your ability to repay the loan (i.e., whether you have some stable source of income, such as money from investments, or if the profitability of your business is stable).

THE SBA, A SMALL BUSINESS'S BEST FRIEND:

The SBA was formed in 1953 to aid small businesses. It can be an invaluable source of information and help for your company.

Contrary to popular belief, the SBA doesn't make loans to small businesses (except in very special circumstances, such as "Disaster Relief Loans"), but it does act as a guarantor of loans.

Suppose you went into a bank looking for a loan for your start-up. The loan officer there would look at your relationship with the bank, your credit history and score, your collateral, your business plan, and the cash flows (or potential cash flows) of your business. In the end, he or she might say, "You're young, you've never run a company full-time before, and you don't have much collateral or a long credit history. We could only loan to you if someone co-signs for your loan." Well, the SBA can fill the shoes of your co-signer in this case.

The SBA isn't a pushover, though: You can't expect to get them to guarantee your loan unless you are a good prospect to begin with. The main benefit of having the SBA in your corner is the opportunity to get better terms on the loan—lower payments or interest rates and longer terms—than you'd be able to get on your own. The SBA isn't in the business of backing loans for people with bad credit or who wouldn't be able to get loans on their own; they can't make a bad credit risk seem good, but they can enhance the attractiveness of a good prospect and help that prospect (you) get better terms for their loan.

The SBA also provides a wide array of useful business support services, such as advice on writing business plans, raising capital, selling your company, and much more. Check them out at www.sba.gov.

Any bank loan officer will be willing to discuss the lending process with you, and that can be a good first step to make if you're considering debt financing for your business. Don't be intimidated by financial professionals and businesspeople. Most of them, especially those working at banks in your community, are there to help people like you, and will usually be very helpful and generous with their time and knowledge if you just ask.

Other Considerations of Debt

Debt obviously has an impact on your business. If you were expecting to have a profit of $5000 a month, you'd have to reduce that amount by the monthly interest payments on your loan. But the loan might be a good way to get the start-up capital you need to purchase important equipment and inventory, rent a facility, or hire someone who will enhance your business.

A couple of good things about debt: The interest payments are tax deductible, so if your company is paying $2000 per year in interest, you can deduct that amount from your taxes in most cases. Also, once the debt is paid, it's gone forever—the lender has no other claim on your business or its profits. This is something that can't be said of equity.

Most people, and most businesses for that matter, never seek to sell ownership, or equity, in their companies. When they need money, they usually take it out of their own pockets or they borrow it from someone. As we've seen above, the process of debt financing is relatively straightforward—you borrow money, and you have to pay it back, usually with some interest.

Selling equity can be much more complicated that taking out a loan. Although it may seem simple to tell someone "I'll sell you 10 percent of my company for $5,000," you could be violating laws and opening yourself up to serious legal consequences by doing that.

Most companies that sell equity either do so by selling it to the general public, something which requires registering with the Securities and Exchange Commission and being subject to a lot of complex rules and requirements. Alternatively, they do what's known as a "private placement" of securities ("securities" is another term for "equity," "stock," or "ownership"). Even a private placement, such as selling a share of your business to a friend, requires that you take a number of steps to comply with state and federal law, create a Private Placement Memorandum (a document containing information about your company, competition, risks associated with the business, and so on), and get investors to complete Subscription Agreements.

As you can see, the process of raising equity capital can seem simple and attractive on the surface, but is actually quite complex and should only be handled with the help of a good securities attorney.

An Alternative to Debt: Equity Financing

"If it's so difficult to sell part of a business, why do so many companies raise money that way?" There are a few answers to this question. First, some smaller companies don't know about the requirements for selling securities, and are running afoul of the law, while some companies are large and can afford to spend the time and money to properly access capital this way. Finally, some companies, both small and large, believe that equity capital is "cheap."

So, ignoring any cost and complexity regarding selling equity in your business, the main incentive for selling equity rather than raising debt for your company is the perception that equity is "cheaper" than debt.

Unlike debt holders and bondholders, equity investors usually won't expect a fixed, or even steady, rate of return on their investment in your business. Instead, the person who has bought stock in a business is usually hoping to see some capital gains—that is, to be able to sell the stock at a higher price in the future (which might come about as your business grows and becomes more profitable). The fact that there's no fixed loan payment being made to equity holders can make equity seem very inexpensive.

Getting money without increasing your liabilities or having to make monthly payments may sound like a very attractive proposition, but realize that equity could turn out to be the most expensive type of capital you'll ever raise.

Suppose you sell 25 percent of your business for $2,500. That might seem great at first, but, down the road, if you're company has become very profitable and is earning $100,000 a year in profits, someone else owns 25 percent, or $25,000, of that. You might come to resent the fact that someone who gave you $2,500 years ago is taking $25,000 a year out of your profits every year now: "I'm doing all the work—all they did was give me some money a long time ago." But that's the cost of equity: when you sell equity, you are selling part of your business, and now it's no longer entirely yours.

There are other reasons that some companies sell equity. Some sell equity to a person or company that gives them not just money, but also some management expertise or access to things the company might not otherwise be able to get (for example, by selling part of your company to a customer, the customer agrees to buy a minimum amount of your product each month, or gives you the clout to negotiate attractive terms with an important supplier). Some sell equity for status; they feel that having an outside owner legitimizes the business. Some sell equity to cash out a bit of what they own—a company's founder might have everything he or she owns tied up in their business, and they diversify by selling a part of the business for enough money to allow them to do other things (buy a house, fund a savings or retirement account, or just get funds to enjoy themselves with).

Wrap-Up: Debt and Equity

Debt and equity are two key sources of external, or outside, financing. For nonprofit companies (and even for some for-profits), grants, donations, gifts, and other sources of outside capital exist.

Most money comes with a cost. The cost can be an amount you have to repay above and beyond the amount you received, or it can come from giving up some ownership of the business you've created. Even many gifts or grants have costs associated with them, but the costs might not be financial -- they might take the form of dependence, influence, obligations to return favors, or recognition. The important thing is to understand what the plusses and minuses of each source of capital are.

Debt is relatively straightforward, and loan officers and other officials at financial lenders can explain any details to you. Equity is much more complex, and should only be considered after consultation with an experienced attorney. Grants and charitable contributions are funding sources that are usually available more to nonprofits and education- or research-driven organizations than to typical start-up companies.

Start by identifying your financial needs, and then examine each alternative for funding that might be available to you. Speak with people who can help you enhance your understanding of raising money—they might be your parents, teachers, friends, bank employees, or local business owners. I've found that if you are open, honest, inquisitive, and respectful, you'll find that the world is full of teachers—you just need to ask for their help.

We're going to leave our friends at Coffee Catering and return to HPK for a look at a Funding Request.

HPK'S FUNDING REQUEST

HPK is seeking $6,000 in capital to fund equipment and inventory purchases. Owners and their family members will contribute $3,000 from personal savings, while the Company is seeking an additional $3,000 in the form of a bank loan.

The main uses of money raised will be the purchase of a used utility van to allow the Company to deliver materials to parties (the Company currently uses a friend's pickup truck, but the availability of that vehicle cannot be guaranteed), the purchase of inventory and equipment, and fees paid to our website developer to enhance the Company's on-line presence.

The Source and Use of Funds Statement is as follows:

Source of Funds	Amount	Use of Funds	Amount
Owner Capital	$ 3,000.00	Website enhancement costs	$ 1,000.00
(see "Ownership Section" of the business plan)		Marketing materials	$ 1,500.00
Bank Loan	$ 3,000.00	Used van for delivery	$ 3,500.00
Total Sources	$ 6,000.00	Total Uses	$ 6,000.00

The Company believes that it will not need to seek additional capital for the foreseeable future, as the business is expected to be cash flow positive from its third month, as detailed in the Financials Section of this Business Plan.

9. Critical Risks

You might think it's strange to point out the risks of your business to someone who might be reading your business plan with the consideration of lending money to your start-up. Shouldn't the business plan focus on the positives, "selling" the reader on the idea, rather than bring things to their attention that might worry them and change their mind about giving you money?

On the surface, that makes sense: you want your plan to explain your business idea, convey your enthusiasm, and convince the reader that you can succeed with the business.

Showing that you understand the risks associated with the business, have identified them, and can discuss plans for dealing with them is a way of demonstrating to the reader that you're being thorough and realistic about things. Every business has some element of risk. If you don't identify the risks associated with your business, the reader of your business plan might think you're unaware of them. That's a dangerous sign.

Be honest with yourself and your business plan reader. You don't need to discuss risks that are overly general (things that are risks to everyone and not just specific to your company – examples would be natural disasters, death, and economic recession), but you do need to point out the things that an intelligent businessperson would be concerned with regarding your company. Here are some examples of business risks:

1. The risk of not having enough capital—there might be a risk that your business runs out of money before it becomes profitable and self-sustaining;

2. The risk of not being able to meet financial targets— maybe because you can't sell as many products as you expected, your selling price turns out to be lower than you thought it would, or costs are higher than you had anticipated;

3. The risk of dependence on one key person, group, or thing—for example, relying upon one supplier for a key part of your product, one employee for a key role, or having a very large part of your sales coming from just one customer;

4. Management risk—if the key people in the company have never worked together before, there is a risk that key personnel won't get along, and could quit (or in the case of younger people, could move or graduate); and

5. Competitive risk—if your company is successful, larger and more established competitors might target your business (they could lower their prices or offer some free service that makes them more competitive), or new companies could arise to challenge you.

Whenever possible, after identifying the risks your business faces, describe ways that your company will address them.

Here's the Business Risk Section of HPK's business plan.

HPK'S BUSINESS RISKS

HPK believes there are three main risks associated with our business:

1. **Weather:** Most of the Company's parties are held outdoors, either in the host family's yard or at reserved sites in public parks. Customers typically book their parties four to six weeks in advance, and the Company offers a 50 percent refund if the event is cancelled due to inclement weather. There is a risk that poor weather can substantially lower the amount of revenue the Company is able to earn. Management has been working on new indoor party themes and venues that could serve as "backup plans," allowing the Company to receive full payment even in the event of poor weather.

2. **Equipment:** The Company relies upon the use of large delivery vehicles (a pickup truck and trailer)

---

that may not be available to the Company at all times. The Company is discussing a vehicle loan from a credit union, and may be able to purchase a truck for business use within six months.

3. **Economic Risk:** Children's parties are discretionary, high-ticket events. Economic weakness could lead more parents to organize parties on their own, or opt for lower-priced alternatives to hosted parties. The Company is working on creating a range of lower-cost party options to address this risk.

10. Exit Strategy or Future Plans

The Exit Strategy is something that most equity investors (such as venture capital companies) are interested in seeing. You don't need to be too concerned about drafting an exit strategy unless you plan to pitch the idea to a VC, but it's possible that anyone making an investment in your business would like to hear about your exit plan.

There are many ways to exit a business: you can close the company, sell all or part of it, merge the business with someone else's firm, or take the company public. The investor putting money into your business simply wants to know if you have a coherent strategy and timeline for exit, and how much money they might make until that point and at that time.

For example, you might say that you're starting the business as a sophomore in high school, and that you plan to exit it by selling the business upon graduation. You explain how you're going to turn the business into something that might be attractive to a potential buyer (maybe a competitor that will be happy to pay you to get your customers, brand, equipment, or other assets; maybe a supplier that's looking to move into the market you've successfully carved a niche in; or maybe to another businessperson who thinks they can "take the company to the next level" or to an employee that wants to be their own boss). You also explain what you think a fair price is (that's a subject that can fill a book in itself, but one idea would be to speak with a local business broker to see if similar businesses have sold, and what price they received), and what the return for the investor would be.

Most companies don't have exit plans, and that's perfectly fine. You might want to run your company indefinitely, maybe handing it down to your kids one day, or you might run it on the side even if you go to college or start a full-time job.

Thinking about an exit—even if you don't plan on actually exiting the business—is important because it forces you to contemplate some important issues. This is particularly true for young entrepreneurs, who need to consider how running the business fits in with their other priorities.

Suppose you start your business when you're sixteen, and by the time you're eighteen the business is booming, taking up all your free time and intruding into all other areas of your life. You find you're not able to hang out with your friends, who will all be graduating and whom you may not see again for a long time; you're not able to take a summer trip to Europe; your grades are suffering; and you can't imagine how you could go to college and run the business at the same time. What if two of your partners are moving out of town after graduation—can you continue the business without them being nearby? What if you're just tired of running everything and want to take a break?

Exits aren't the only option for someone that's become a victim of their own success, but the other options — such as hiring and training someone else to take over and run the day-to-day aspects of the business while you pursue other goals — can require much more advanced planning than simply folding tent or selling out.

The process of thinking about what happens if the business is very successful down the road is more important than answering the specific question of what your exit strategy is.

Here's how HPK addresses future plans and exit strategy in their business plan.

HPK'S FUTURE PLANS AND EXIT STRATEGY

The Company believes it will continue growing beyond the involvement of the four original founders, and has crafted a growth strategy that addresses the changes in management that we anticipate.

Three of the four founding partners of HPK are beginning their senior year in high school, while the fourth partner is beginning her junior year. Next year, it is possible that one of the founding partners, Trinity, will move out of state for college, but three of the other founders will remain in Springfield. Jordan is likely to attend Springfield University, but plans to continue working part-time for the Company. Ariel plans to work full-time for the Company after high school. Bailey will continue working part-time during the school year and full-time during weekends and holidays.

The founders of the Company plan to hire a professional manager within nine months of start-up. This manager will work closely with the founders, learning the business and helping to implement new growth strategies, such as organizing parties for teens, corporate clients, and others.

> Although management anticipates operating the Company for the foreseeable future, discussions with a business broker in Springfield indicate that a business of our nature with strong growth prospects (20 percent net profit growth per year for at least five years) should be able to sell for 1.25–1.5 times annual revenues. We estimate revenues in Year Five of our business to be $300,000, indicating a potential exit value of $375,000 to $450,000 at that time, should an exit be sought.

11. The Executive Summary

Now that we've gone through all the business plan sections in detail, let's put the executive summary together. Remember the checklist of items that should be in the summary:

- A profile of the company, with mission statement

- The nature of the business and its product/service

- Information on the industry the business is in

- Goals

- Source and use of funds (this can be omitted in the Summary and shown elsewhere.)

- Financial summary (this can also be included elsewhere.)

- Exit strategy and/or future plans

Here's the Executive Summary of Healthy Parties for Kids, LLC.

HPK'S EXECUTIVE SUMMARY

Twenty-five percent of children between the ages of six and twelve in this country are obese, and the rate of childhood diabetes has more than doubled in the last twenty years. Parents want their kids to eat healthy foods and get outside to play, but often throw these values out the window during special occasions like birthday parties.

Healthy Parties for Kids, LLC ("HPK"), was set up to plan and deliver nutritional party alternatives to young people. Our mission is to improve the health of children and ease the burdens of busy parents by organizing and hosting healthy and enjoyable gatherings for children.

We offer fun and healthy parties and events for people between the ages of one and 14.

The children's birthday party market in the U.S. is estimated to be a $10 billion industry that should grow to over $20 billion in the next five years. We target families with a median income of $75,000 near the downtown area, and estimate that there are over 50,000 kids in our target market.

HPK provides convenience and peace of mind for parents, while entertaining their children with fun, active games and providing them with nutritious, enjoyable foods and drinks.

In less than ten minutes, parents can choose from a set of party options on our web site, selecting from a variety of budgets, activities, and themes. A few clicks and it's done: HPK takes over, mailing invitations and thank-you cards, buying and preparing treats, setting up and taking down decorations, leading kids through games and events, and explaining the importance of making nutrition and physical fitness a part of their everyday lives. Parents can rest easy knowing that the organization and management of their child's important day are in good hands. Mom and Dad can spend their time enjoying the day and creating memories with their children.

Competition for our company is sparse, with only a small number of companies focusing on parties for young people. A typical birthday party at one of our competitors runs $425 on average, but parents complain about the "rush and routine" at these places. Aside from our basic, healthy-party approach, HPK has many advantages over our competitors:

- **We are affordable**—about 20 percent cheaper than our average competitor.

- **We are flexible**—we can accommodate many dates and times.

- **We are familiar**—we are members of the community and have worked with many kids and their parents.

- **We are local**—we are not a chain with a "one-size-fits all" approach to events.

- **We are timely**—we address a pressing need in the market, at a critical time.

Our company provides affordable, safe, and fun parties for kids, with special attention devoted to each party and child. We offer a range of healthy foods and fun activities, and our staff engages with the children, using their names, talking about their favorite characters, and giving them quality time and attention. Most parties are held at the parents' home or in public parks, and we encourage outdoor play and activity.

With four founders and a large group of responsible and trained friends and helpers, we are able to offer up to three different parties in three locations at any given date and time, meaning that three kids with the same birthday can each be accommodated.

Our business was formed and is run by four high school friends. We have years of experience in dealing with children through our babysitting jobs, and have tested the kid party planning concept for over six months. We are ready to launch in the beginning of May, and will be fully functional by the start of school summer vacation, a key time for children's outdoor birthday parties. We are seeking an additional investment or loan of $3,000 to purchase business supplies and a vehicle. We believe that HPK can grow to $300,000 of sales and $60,000 of profits within five years of start-up.

Going forward, we anticipate opportunities to expand the business into teen and corporate parties and events, form a partnership with a local food company that would allow us to create our own brand of pre-made healthy entrees for kids, and franchise the business nationwide. The founders expect to run the business indefinitely, working while in college and after graduation.

In just a few pages, the girls behind HPK explained their service, the need for it, the absence of good alternatives, how they're different from their competitors, and the value proposition they offer to parents (low cost + healthy + peace of mind).

They show they've done their homework, doing simple market studies, questionnaires and surveys, demographic research on the target market, and studying the critical success factors of the business and customer decision-making criteria.

A summary of your product and service, such as the HPK one above, can be not only informative, but a persuasive sales document to anyone considering lending your company money or investing in it, agreeing to be a partner or critical supplier, or just trying to decide if they should use your company's service versus a competitor's.

The appendixes are the place to include data on things you think would be helpful to explain the business and its approach to an unfamiliar reader. You don't want to jam this section with dense material that few people are likely to read. Rather, fill it with pertinent and easy-to-digest information, such as the following:

- Detailed biographies of management and key team members

- Samples of promotional materials

- Testimonials and press write-ups

- Findings from market research, such as survey results

- Pictures of key things associated with the business (can be a picture of the product, a factory, store or event)

- Detailed financial models

- Any key legal documents you wish to disclose, such as lease agreements for business property, a copy of your operating agreement, and copies of contracts with distributors

- Information on service providers (e.g., info on tax preparer, attorney, consultants, contractors, etc.)

- Pertinent articles or news on the industry

- Detailed competitive analysis or market analysis

- Copies of any patents, trademarks, or any other protection of intellectual property

- Copies of business licenses or other legal documents

- Copies of letters of intent from suppliers or customers

12. *Final Steps with the Business Plan & Other Things to Add*

Make a table of contents to put into the business plan. You can place it after the cover sheet, or right after the executive summary.

If there are trade or business secrets or sensitive information that you don't want disclosed included in your business plan, you should ask viewers to sign a non-disclosure agreement (you can find samples online). Don't be overzealous with this -- you don't want to act like you're protecting national secrets just to make yourself feel important, but if there are truly sensitive data in the business plan, you may ask the reader to sign an NDA.

It would be a good idea to have page numbers on your business plan (so you can easily tell someone "refer to page 15 for that information"). You should also put the company name and contact information in the "footer" of each page (for example, "HPK, LLC, contact: Trinity@HPK.com). Finally, it's perfectly fine to add photos, flash, or other add-ins to your business plan; just be sure that anything you add complements the plan (i.e., makes it easier for the reader to understand what you've written about), rather than just adding "bling" to it.

Finally, try to stay organized. You should record information about business plans that go out: Who received one, from whom, when, and what the response (if any) was. Make sure that there is follow-up contact from someone in your company to the person or people that received the plan.

Chapter 10:

Other Types of Plans

While the business plan is the most well known and popular type of plan for a start-up, there are a number of other plans and processes that you're encouraged to go through. Fortunately, none of these are as intensive and time-consuming as the business plan is.

As we saw earlier, starting a successful business is a lot more than just trying to maximize opportunity; it's also about minimizing risk. Let's take a look at how to do Risk Management Planning.

Risk Management Planning

Risk management planning (RMP) can be fairly simple, and you've already used some of the methods that would be involved in it. You've hopefully already done the brainstorming exercise to identify major risks that were described earlier. You may have come up with a list of risks and some ways to minimize them.

Let's look at two other things that can help you in RMP: making contingency plans and diversifying elements in your business. We'll also look at operating agreements, and how they help reduce business risks.

Contingency Planning

Contingency planning is simply the process of making plans for "what-if" events. For example, you can make plans for every what-if risk you've identified for the organic vegetable delivery business described earlier in this book. What if the farmer supplying you with produce isn't able to bring a shipment in one week? In that case, your contingency plan might be to have one of the farmer's neighbors drive the truck down for an extra fee or to pay someone you work with to drive over and pick up the vegetables.

Having contingency plans for every major risk your business may face is an important part of risk management planning. Diversification is another tool that can help mitigate risk.

Diversification

Diversification is simply "spreading your bets." Your business is going to be much riskier if it relies on one supplier, one large customer, one delivery person, and one manager than if it has multiple sources of each input. Being too diversified can create its own headaches, though—lack of focus or too many suppliers to manage. You should always try to have at least two sources of every critical success factor, which means two suppliers, customers, and so on.

The Operating Agreement

An Operating Agreement, or OA, isn't a plan, it's a document, but a lot of planning goes into it, and it goes a long way toward reducing your risk and potential problems if you're starting a company with partners. The OA outlines the roles and responsibilities of each person involved in the business. It also explains how decisions are made, what reports are kept, and what people involved with the business can and can't do.

The OA isn't an employee manual, which outlines procedures for company employees (and may be something you'll need only in the future, after your business has grown beyond just you and one or two partners). The OA is a higher-level document that addresses things like the following:

- What types of decisions are put to a vote, and how the vote is counted (e.g., If there are three partners, does each partner have an equal vote, or does the weight of each vote depend on how much money each partner has put into the business or how many hours they've worked?)

- Which decisions require unanimous consent, and which require just a simple majority?

- What happens to a partner's share of the business if he/she leaves the company, is incapacitated, or just fails to do his or her job?

- Does a partner have the right to work in another, similar, business "on the side," or does that create a potential conflict of interest—something that might put that partner's own interest ahead of the company's?

- What's the process for determining if a new partner should be admitted? What happens if two partners want a friend to join and the other partner is against it?

- Does a partner have the right to borrow money in the company's name on his/her own? Make donations to charity in the company's name? Sign contracts without consulting the other partners?

The list goes on and on. Again, many people skip this important stage because they set up businesses with friends or family members and figure "we can work something out" if a situation arises. Of course, it rarely works that way. One partner might concede to a decision the other partner wants, thinking that his friend owes him one next time, and then boils over when his "favor" isn't returned. Often, one partner might contribute $500 cash to the business and the other can put in only $250; does the ownership of 50/50 change based on that? What if the partner that put in $250 also did ten hours more work for the company than the partner that put in $500—how is the value of that work determined? You can see incidents that might seem easy to work out in theory can become hard to address fairly when it comes to a specific situation.

The OA should be created with the input of all partners (at least all partners that might be active in running the business), and each should sign and keep a copy of it.

In the future, if there is any dispute or confusion about an issue, you can refer to the OA to see what you all agreed to up front. This makes problems much easier to deal with, as a cold, hard contract takes most of the personal and emotional factors out of the equation. It could also prevent nasty and costly legal issues, such as one partner suing another.

The Stress Test

Aside from the financial statements and plans you make for your business, you need to do some personal financial planning and preparation.

Consider how your business plans could affect your personal finances. Suppose you expect to spend $500 you've saved up to start your company, and another $500 over the first three months of operations before your business gets enough customers to break even or earn a profit. By the sixth month of operations, you're expecting to be making $1,000 a month from your business, or about $20 an hour.

Stress testing is the process of putting your plans through different "stressful" scenarios. Assume, for example, that your business eats up more money than you had expected, or doesn't break even as quickly as you had anticipated. Run the numbers in your forecasts and see if you can survive without the $1,000 of income you're expecting in six months. Do you have enough of a financial cushion to take you through the tough times if the company doesn't grow as expected? If not, you might consider saving up more money before launching the business, starting on a smaller scale, getting more start-up and operating capital through a loan, or other responses to the results of your stress test.

The basic purpose of the stress test is to ensure that you and your business can survive bad-case scenarios, and how long you could last if the business takes longer than expected to start paying for itself.

Final Word: Do You Ever Not Need a Plan?

I can think of two cases in which detailed planning is not necessary.

If you intend to launch a small sole proprietorship (a one-person company) that you don't expect to grow dramatically, you can probably launch without any detailed planning. If you want to simply start mowing lawns for people after school, you don't necessarily need to spend a lot of time researching and planning. If you're planning to run a company in which you and three friends offer lawn care services to people however, then some planning would be in order (an operating agreement would be advised, as would some consideration of risk management, advertising, and other areas).

Second, if you're launching a business that is very easy to start (and end), you don't expect to take any outside funding (no loans or investments from others), and you can easily churn and burn through variations of the business, you don't necessarily need formal plans.

Suppose you want to create simple applications for smart phones. You're going to take an approach of "throwing a bunch of stuff on the wall and seeing what sticks," meaning that you're going to design an app and see if people start using it; if they don't, no big deal, you just make another app. In this type of business, it might take you a lot longer to make a business plan than it would to actually make and test five different applications. Since you're able to back out of any app that doesn't work without much cost and move on to the next app, and since you're not pitching your idea to outside funding sources, a business plan might take more work than it's worth. If, however, you want to start a company with a few partners or employees that will work together to create apps and might need a loan to rent a workspace, buy some PCs and rent a T-1 line, then you should go through the formal planning process.

Part 4:

Launching Your Business

Chapter 11:

The Mechanics of Launching

Congratulations! You've made it through the planning phase and are now ready to officially launch your business. By taking the time to do the planning that was detailed in the previous section, you've done more than most entrepreneurs already, and have greatly increased your chances of success.

Now you're ready to set up your company. The real work is the planning that goes into a company and, later, the work of actually running it (a subject for a different book). The good news is that the actual setting up of your business is usually straightforward, standardized, and fairly easy. Let's look at the key steps and considerations for this stage.

STEPS FOR SETTING UP A COMPANY:

1. Register the Company.

2. Apply for an EIN.

3. Register the business with your state's government.

4. Obtain any licenses or permits necessary for the business.

5. Open accounts in the Company's name.

6. Identify and select service providers (tax, legal, accounting).

7. Secure other things necessary for the business (storefront, equipment, inventory).

8. Start working!

---

1. Registering the Company

You will need to register your business's name with government agencies, and use that legal name on all forms, applications, licenses, and permits. It's possible to do business under a different name from the official company name, but this requires a "Doing Business As" ("DBA," also known as a "fictitious name," "trade name," or "assumed name") registration.

For example, you can register your company name as "Rogers & Smith Lawn Care, LLC," but do business as "A-1 Lawn Care."

It's not necessary to have two separate names (an "official" one and a DBA one), but some companies prefer to, and registering a DBA is easy. You will need to check your state's requirements for registering a company and a fictitious name: Some states require registering with the state government, some with the county, and some require registration of the company name but not the fictitious one. In California, for example, a for-profit company doing business in a name other than the owner's full legal name must file a Fictitious Name Statement with the County Recorder-Clerk's Office in the county in which business will be conducted.

Registering a company and a fictitious name can usually be done online, or with forms available online. The process of registration takes only a few minutes, though you will probably have to pay a registration fee.

2. Getting an EIN

EIN stands for "Employer Identification Number" (also known as an Employer Tax ID or Form SS-4), and is like a company's Social Security Number.

You can obtain an EIN from the IRS (go to www.irs.gov) or apply for an EIN online. It's a simple process of filling out some basic information on the business and owner.

3. Registering with the State Revenue Agency

This is another step that is generally quick and painless. Your EIN is a federal ID number. You also need to obtain tax IDs and permits from the state your business is located in. Some businesses are required to collect sales taxes from the sale of their products, and those companies will need a sales tax permit or vendor license from the state or local government, if not both.

The site www.business.gov has a lot of useful information on the license and permit requirements for various businesses in different states.

4. Obtaining Licenses and Permits

Most businesses require some type of business license or permit to operate legally. Most small businesses need just a general business license from state and local government agencies, but the requirements vary from state to state.

Again, www.business.gov is a good place to find information specific to your state and business type.

5. Opening Business Accounts

You can take a copy of your company registration documents and your EIN to a bank or other financial institution and open business checking, savings, or other accounts.

This leads to an aside on the importance of not mingling personal funds and business funds.

SEPARATE BUSINESS AND PERSONAL FUNDS

You will need to make sure that you don't mingle personal and business funds. This is why you should have separate checking accounts and credit cards for yourself and your business. You can deduct business expenses from your company taxes, but you have to be careful not to add personal expenses in your business accounts, or vice versa.

Having only one account for both you and your business creates a lot of work to untangle and sort out your expenses at tax time. For another thing, you could be hit with fines and penalties if the IRS ever audits you and finds that you're mixing personal and business accounts. Some basic accounting software, such as QuickBooks, can help make your day-to-day accounting relatively painless.

Another thing to consider is the division of certain expenses. If you have an office at home, you can take a home office deduction, and you can write off (deduct as a business expense) a portion of your utility and other bills. For example, if your home office takes up 20 percent of the total area of your home, you might be able to deduct 20% of your heating and electrical bill as a business expense. You'll want to consult with your tax advisor for issues like this.

(Note:"Home office" deductions are a big red flags to the IRS, and could prompt an audit. If you are using a room in your home as an office, you should make sure that room is not used for anything else; it's not a good idea to set up a desk and computer in your living room and try to call that your home office.)

Don't make the mistake of running your business through your personal checking, credit card, or savings accounts and thinking you can disentangle things later. The process of sorting out business and personal expenses when everything's on one account is a lot more difficult and time-consuming than it may seem, and there's no reason to create extra work for yourself. By clearly separating the business's finances from the owner's personal ones, you'll save yourself a tremendous amount of work and trouble.

6. Finding Service Providers

Most people who start small companies don't have the budget to bring in a lot of expert help for things like accounting and bookkeeping, legal services, tax preparation, and other areas. If you start off small, you should be able to navigate tax and legal codes on your own, and can handle your own bookkeeping and accounting just by being organized and using a computer program like QuickBooks.

Even if you have some money that could go toward professional services, it's a good idea to at least try to do some of these things yourself. For one thing, professional fees are usually very high (a good lawyer can charge $500 or more an hour). Plus, you'll get a lot of experience by putting some time into learning the basics of managing your own books, doing your own taxes, and researching legal and other issues on your own.

When you do need outside help, look online at sites that give small businesspeople free advice. You can also check agencies like the Small Business Administration for help. Look at your network of friends, relatives, and associates. It's said that there are no more than six degrees of separation between you and anyone else in the world; you might not know an attorney who would give you some good free advice, but your parents, neighbor, teacher, or a local business owner you know might. Also, some businesses, such as Costco, offer business services such as payroll and credit card processing to their members at reasonable prices.

After you've tried to handle things yourself, done some investigation for answers online, and picked the brains of people you know that have some expertise on the subject matter, you may have no other choice than to go to a professional and get some help. Most professionals will give you an initial free consultation to hear about your business needs, will let you know if they can help you or not, and explain how much you can expect to pay for their services.

Don't be shy about asking questions: You're the customer, and they're the person looking for another client. Don't be intimidated or frightened because you're "just a kid" and they're an older, experienced pro. Most of these people will admire your ambition and will do their best to be fair and open with you. They know a 17-year-old with a start-up company isn't their meal ticket, so you usually don't need to worry about them trying to take advantage of you. Ask them if they have the time to handle the job you've described, if they have experience with the type of job you're asking about, and what their best estimate of a cost is.

You can check these people out on sites like Yelp or LinkedIn, and with the Better Business Bureau. If they seem honest and you feel they could be a good long-term advisor for you and your business, then go ahead and hire them. A good professional can cost a lot, but can save you a lot more by making sure things are being done the way they should be (for example, that you're getting all the tax deductions you're entitled to, and pay-ing the taxes you need to).

7. *Securing Other Things Necessary to the Business*

Each company has its own unique needs. Some busi-nesses are purely "virtual," with no office space, people work-ing online from various locations, and no special equipment or inventory necessary to keep the organization functioning. An example of this type of business might be a website design company whose founders work from home, creating websites and interacting with clients through e-mails and teleconfer-ences.

But even a virtual business like the one described above needs some "procurement planning". For example, the two founders, who work together on website design, might need to have dedicated high-speed internet connections put into their home offices. They might need newer computers to do their jobs more effectively, dedicated business phone lines for cus-tomers to call into, and design software that would help them make their product more competitive.

For a business such as a coffee shop, the list of necessary items can be lengthy: you need to lease a retail site, buy special commercial-grade equipment, lease a commercial dishwasher, order uniforms, set up contracts with companies that will deliver fresh pastries to your shop every morning, buy food and beverage products and special cleaning materials, get approval from the fire marshal, get training in food handling, and a host of other things.

I'll assume that you've had some experience in the type of business you're planning to start (most people who open their own coffee shops have spent a lot of time working in other coffee shops and know how to operate the business), or that you can scale up your company gradually (i.e., start a lawn-care firm with just your truck, a lawnmower, and a few pieces of other equipment, and then add things as the business grows).

If you're thinking about starting a business that you haven't had much experience with already, especially if that business requires a lot of start-up capital, you should make it a point to speak to a few businesspeople that have experience in the type of company you want to open. You might think that a person running a bagel shop downtown wouldn't want to speak with someone who might open a store on the other end of town, and you could be right. But I've found that people who set up and are running their own small businesses are open to telling their story, and like to talk about their companies the way new parents like to talk about their baby. If you approach these people with respect and seriousness and do your homework in advance of talking with them (i.e., you've done your planning), they will be quick to recognize that you're not just some teenager with a naïve dream, but a person that genuinely cares for the same type of thing they do.

For a business that requires inventory and equipment, there's a delicate balance between having too much and too little. You don't want to spend $10,000 on equipment only to find out that you only needed half of the things you bought; conversely, you wouldn't want to be stuck turning customers away at noon because your restaurant didn't stock enough meat or bread to make the sandwiches you're selling. Market research can help you get this balance right, but speaking with some experienced businesspeople can be invaluable in helping you get off on the right foot.

8. Blast Off

Once you've done your planning and gone through the mechanics of setting up your company and getting any equipment, supplies, and help you need to run it, then there's nothing left to do but launch.

A launch can be a big event, such as the grand opening of a restaurant, or something that is low-key or entirely inconspicuous. In any case, you're now officially a business owner and entrepreneur. Congratulations! The things you've learned to this point, and the things you'll learn over the course of running your business — whether it's a success or failure — will be a form of education and experience that will be useful to you in just about anything you do with your life. You have created something from nothing. You've identified a problem and have acted boldly to present a solution for it. Even if you fail, you've acted; that's what an entrepreneur does, and that's what makes them special.

Hopefully, you'll have a general set of plans for three main conditions: what to do if things are fantastic (i.e., growing your business without sacrificing quality or the other things that made your business a success in the first place); what to do if things are just so-so (i.e., running the business if it doesn't live up to your original expectations); and what to do if things are bad.

In our final section, we'll look at what happens in this third scenario.

Chapter 12:

Knowing When to Surrender

According to Census data, nearly 70 percent of new businesses formed in the year 2000 survived at least two years, and over 50 percent survived for five or more years. Despite these good rates of survivorship (I won't say "success rates," because many of these survivors might not be very successful — not making enough money to make the ventures worthwhile to their founders, and just "hanging on"), many businesses do fail.

Small business failures can be due to any number of things: the owners found something better to do, or weren't really interested in the business in the first place; the forecasts for income were too optimistic and the owners spent a lot on the business, never to see the income they hoped for materialize; a new competitor entered the area and drove others out of business; or the owners felt their opportunity costs for being entrepreneurs were too high, and decided they would rather be employees of a larger company.

Failures can come about by defeat or by surrender. Defeats are pretty clear—you don't make enough money to pay the bills, and you're shut down. Surrendering can require a lot more thought and, perhaps surprisingly to many people, more character than either succeeding or being defeated. The decision to quit will usually come about because the person behind the business becomes disillusioned that the reality of running a firm is a lot less glamorous than the dream; they get burned out and begin questioning their decision to go the entrepreneurial route in the first place. In most cases, the business owner could continue for a while longer, maybe even for years, but once the passion is gone and the doubts have set in, it's probably time to walk away.

A more difficult surrender occurs when the passion and the dreams remain, but the business is losing more money than anticipated. I've seen people with a lot of passion and a complete belief in the product or service they were offering stay on board sinking ships, refusing to give up and, worse, putting more and more of their personal assets into the failing firm. Watching a company go under is a painful thing; watching it take down assets that should have been kept separate from the business—the safety net of the founders, in many cases—is much worse. People who let their faith in the company cost them not only what they originally budgeted for the business, but also their homes and cars, their college and retirement savings, and everything they own are dangers to themselves.

When you set out to start a business, make not only a budget and financial plan, but plans with some "milestones" and "limits" in them. Milestones are key events that you expect your business to experience at different stages, or goals you hope to achieve. They're the ground marks that show if you're on, ahead, or behind plan. Use these milestones to adjust your plan. In some cases, you might be so far off a key milestone that you need to go back to square one and chart a new direction, or even realize that your business just isn't working out.

You might set milestones of reaching $100,000 in sales in your first year, having 20 employees by your second year, and launching two new products with sales of $100,000 each in your third year. Eighteen months into your business, if you're at $40,000 of revenues with two employees, you probably need to greatly reassess your business and ask yourself if you'll be content being a very small company that may never achieve the level of success that led you to launch in the first place. Are the opportunity costs of running your own business worth the amount it's paying you? In other words, are you giving up more to be an entrepreneur than you're getting from the experience?

Limits are at the other end of the spectrum from milestones. Limits are conditions you set for yourself and your firm — lines in the sand that you vow not to cross. For example, you might say, "If the losses of the company ever total $50,000, I'll shut it down" or "I'm willing to make infusions of cash into the business if it's struggling, but those owner contributions will never total more than $10,000 and I'll never touch my family's long-term assets." Walking away from a business is a difficult endeavor. Many entrepreneurs look at the companies they've set up as their children: They've given birth to a firm; raised it; helped it through difficulties; and remained committed to it. Giving up on a "child," as these businesspeople see it, is out of the question. They make excuses for not hitting milestones, and justifications for casting aside any limits they had imposed.

That is a fatal attitude.

Businesses can be opened and closed quite easily in most circumstances, and you can always take what you've learned from a failed business and make a much more successful second attempt later on.

There comes a point at which cold, dispassionate reason becomes a greater asset than passion and perseverance. As explained earlier, your greatest asset might be your youth -- you can make big mistakes and lose everything when you're young and still have a long career to make up for your errors. But as you get older, your room for error lessens. If you're going to make big mistakes, it's best to make them when you're young. Still, setting milestones and adhering to pre-set limits on your business can prevent you from making very costly errors and prevent tremendous amounts of pain and suffering.

The Mechanics of Closing a Business

Whether you're a sole proprietor running a business out of your bedroom, or a CEO running a large corporation from a big corner office, there are a number of things you need to do to officially and completely close your company. You will need to officially dissolve your business so that you don't have to pay business taxes or make additional tax filings (after the year your business is dissolved) and to protect yourself from lawsuits and the possibility of another company using your name to incur debts you might be liable for.

Here's a checklist of steps to take in order to close your company:

1. A sole proprietor can decide to close the company on his or her own; a partnership, LLC, or corporation will need to have a vote to close the business. You will need to follow the procedures set out in your organizational documents or the laws of the state your business is in. Based on the state you're in, you may need a majority of the owners, a supermajority (such as 2/3 or 3/4) of owners, or even the unanimous approval of owners to approve the closure the company. Make a record of the decision, with written consent of the owners. Keep this record on file after the business is dissolved. This will protect you from one of the business owners coming after you in court or using the business for his or her own purposes (such as incurring debts in the company name after it's dissolved).

2. Pay any taxes your business owes, and remember that you'll need to file a tax return for the final year of your company's existence. The IRS can hold owners of a company personally liable for payroll and other taxes, even if you're operating as an LLC or corporation, so it is very important that you don't think that closing the business means you don't have to pay your taxes or file returns.

3. Notify your local government office (most likely, the secretary of state or a division of that office) that your business is closing. You will probably need to file forms, such as a "certificate of dissolution," to officially dissolve your business. You may be required to provide proof that all your business taxes have been paid in order to close your business. Your local government office will help you cancel your business license.

4. Contact any agencies that issued licenses or permits to your company, such as a seller's permit or permit to use a fictitious name. Notify them of your business's closure and have them cancel all outstanding permits and licenses for your company.

5. Notify creditors that you are going to close the business. You will need to either pay off these creditors in full or negotiate a settlement with them for business debts. When you've paid off a creditor or agreed upon a settlement, get a letter from them indicating that you have no further obligations to them.

6. Contact service providers and suppliers to notify them of your upcoming closure. Suppliers will want to know when their last deliveries should be made or if you're going to return any merchandise. Service providers, such as utility companies, will need to know when the last day of service to your company will be.

7. Close all business bank accounts and cancel all business credit cards.

8. Start working on collecting any money you're owed immediately; it may be much harder to collect money owed to your company once the company has shut down.

9. If your business has a landlord, you will need to follow the notification period in your lease document. You will be responsible for fulfilling your contractual obligations, which may mean paying rent until the end of the lease period, though you may be able to negotiate terms with your landlord.

10. If your business has employees, you should give them at least two weeks' notice of the business closure. You can inform key employees, who might have to help in the closure, earlier.

11. Inform your customers that you will be closing, and explain how you will fill final orders. Return any deposits or funds from unfilled orders to your customers.

12. You should put an announcement in your local newspaper stating that the business is closing. This will protect you from being on the hook for any future actions by a business with the same name as the one you're closing; it allows creditors to know that your company can no longer incur business debts.

13. Give all relevant parties—suppliers, customers, and government agencies—your new contact information.

14. Make sure you keep all business records. Some records, such as tax returns, construction permits, and trademark licenses, should be kept forever; others, such as deposit slips and bank statements, need be held for only three years. The rule of thumb is "when in doubt, keep the records for seven years." A certified public accountant (CPA), state or local agencies (such as your secretary of state or county clerk), or the IRS can provide further guidance.

One final note: if you have to close your company because you're unable to pay your bills and cannot meet your obligations to creditors, then bankruptcy could be a consideration. It's beyond the scope of this book to go through the ins and outs of business bankruptcies. You should consult with a local bankruptcy attorney for help with this avenue.

Conclusion

Starting a business is an adventure. It can be scary, stressful, and painful, but it can also be extremely rewarding on many different levels. In this book, I've tried to show you three general things:

1. Just about anyone can start a business. You don't need a lot of money; you don't need to be a financial or computer genius. Don't let the idea of starting a business intimidate you.

2. While nearly anyone can start a business, not everyone can succeed. Being successful requires a good idea, thorough planning, adequate resources, hard work, good execution, and luck. Too many entrepreneurs think that a good idea alone will be enough, but that's rarely the case; planning is an area that's often neglected, but which can give your company an edge over others.

3. There are few things you can do when you are young that are as rewarding as starting your own company. Starting up and running a company will give you a higher quality education in all aspects of business—management, marketing, finance, accounting, human resources, strategy, operations, and more—than just about any endeavor. Running a business will teach you about yourself, forge character, and create capabilities that will be assets to you for the rest of your life. In that

respect, there is no failure for the entrepreneur that plans and prepares properly; the only failure is the experience that doesn't teach you valuable lessons.

Entrepreneurship isn't for everyone, but if you believe it's the right path for you, plan wisely and good luck with your venture.

A Special Chapter for Parents: What You Can Do to Help Your Teen Understand Money and Business

Many parents have asked me what they can do to encourage an interest in business in their children. If you're the parent of a child or teen who is already interested in business, congratulations! Your son or daughter has taken an interest in something productive and useful, and the knowledge they acquire about money and business will help them for the rest of their lives. Your kids are clean slates when it comes to money, able to avoid the financial problems that plague many adults and capitalize on the opportunities that exist for enterprising and ambitious young people.

If your child isn't terribly interested in business, it's probably because the subject hasn't been presented to them properly. A teenager might not get excited about the idea of saving money for six months in order to buy a big item they want, and might think that any planning—such as making a budget and savings plan—that goes into something like this would be boring. Your teenager might be more interested, though, in knowing how to create their own record label, market their own line of jewelry, or turn a part-time job of mowing lawns or babysitting into a business that might pay them twenty times more than they're making now for the same amount of work.

The best ways to create or foster an interest in finance and business in your kids are to show an interest in the subjects yourself, model good financial behavior, and involve your kids in household finances. Here's a short list of things you can do to get your teen interested in money and business, or to help them expand on an interest they might already have.

1. Don't assume they'll figure it out for themselves.

Giving your teen an allowance and letting them make their own financial decisions is probably a necessary—but insufficient—approach to giving them a solid financial education. Unfortunately, this is the extent to which many parents involve themselves in the subject.

Many parents blithely assume that their teen has gotten it all figured out when it comes to money, until that fateful day when Junior calls to tell them he's buried under $15,000 of credit card debt and doesn't know what to do: He plans to drop out of school and move back into his old room, and hopes that you can send him a big check to help bail him out! "But Junior, wasn't the allowance enough to teach you all you needed to know about money?"

Money is a responsibility, and some people need help accepting and managing that responsibility.

2. Involve yourself in your child's business education.

If you do not involve yourself in your children's financial and business education, you are depriving them of their best financial resource: an experienced, caring, and helpful teacher.

Studies have shown that parents are more uncomfortable speaking with their kids about money than about sex. Money isn't something parents should be uneasy speaking to their kids about: All of us have made mistakes in money or business, but opening up and talking with your child about lessons you've learned—or sharing experiences about successes you've had—can be very rewarding. Your teen might appreciate that you're speaking with them as an adult about important issues they'll face in their adult lives (such as the lure and potential danger of credit cards, what to expect when they enter the workforce, or how to make and follow a budget).

Many parents don't discuss money with their teenagers because they're embarrassed by their own financial situation or lack of knowledge about important financial concepts. If that's the case, then you have an opportunity to bond with your teen by studying money and business together. It's never too late to learn, and taking this educational journey with your child can be enlightening and rewarding in many ways.

Some parents avoid financial discussions because they don't want to cause their teen stress, opening up about tough subjects that the child might have no control over. Consider that the stress of your child making their own financial mistakes and having to dig themselves out of a hole could be much greater than the stress you'd feel by involving your kids in discussions about money.

Finally, some parents don't talk about money with their kids because they simply believe it's none of their business. I think that's the attitude of a bygone era. Today—when kids are besieged by offers for credit cards the moment they turn eighteen, when record numbers of young people are filing for bankruptcy, and when a young person's access to money is greater than ever before and the consequences of mismanaging it can be severe—it is more important than ever that parents take the responsibility of teaching their kids about money seriously.

A final and important word on this subject: Don't lecture your kids; speak to them as you would to an adult. Your kids are a lot smarter than you might think they are, and though they might not know about a subject like business when you first start talking with them about it, you'll be surprised by how quickly they can learn.

3. Model good behavior.

Your child is more likely to develop a healthy attitude toward money and an intellectual curiosity about it if you, the parent, isn't constantly complaining about it ("Where does all our money go? Why aren't we ever able to save anything?") or griping about business stories you see on the news ("The government's using my tax dollars to bail out rich bankers").

Take an inquisitive and unbiased approach toward the subject of money and business and your kids are likely to do the same. Recognize chances to talk about money: The next time you're watching the news and a story about interest rates or inflation comes on, ask your son or daughter if they know how something like that would affect them; at a restaurant, see if you and your teen can work out how much profit the restaurant is making off of your $50 dinner.

Don't live beyond your means; create and maintain a budget (and involve your teen in making and tracking it). Save and invest what you can (and show your teen the difference between saving and investing; have him or her sit down with you each month to go through your bank statement or investment reports). Show them the real cost of owning something like a car (not just the cost of buying the car itself, but the cost of insuring it, maintaining it, buying gas, and the loss you'll have—an introduction to depreciation—when you sell it in the future).

4. Help and encourage your teen.

There are many ways to encourage your teenager to learn more about business and money.

Don't Give Them a Fish—Teach Them How to Fish

When I was young, if I wanted a new bicycle, my dad used to help me come up with ideas for how to earn the money to buy one myself. We'd brainstorm ideas for earning what I'd need, talk about the plusses and minuses of each idea, and then he might tell me how best to get started on the idea that I settled on. By covering the necessities (food, shelter, and clothing) of your teen's life but helping her with ideas to pay for her own luxuries (an expensive pair of shoes, a new game system or cell phone, a trip with her friends), you could help your teen learn some important financial and business lessons.

Work Together

Create financial projects that you and your teen can work on together. You could make a household budget or savings plan with your teen. Try to create a project that you can monitor the progress of with weekly meetings, and that will last between one and three months (longer, and your teen might lose interest).

Plan Field Trips

A financial field trip with your teen—or better yet, a series of trips—can be a great way for you and your child to learn about money and business together, and can be easy to arrange.

Ask a bank loan officer if they would be willing to meet with you and your son or daughter for an hour to explain what their job, the types of people they meet, how they decide whom to loan money to, and how much they'll lend.

Ask the owner of a local business you like or admire if they would meet you and your teen to explain the challenges and rewards of setting up and running their own business or non-profit organization.

Set up a meeting with your local Chamber of Commerce, a business broker or attorney, a representative of the Small Business Association, a tax accountant, a small business consultant, a venture capitalist, or any number of other businesspeople or organizations. The list is nearly endless, and you and your teen will probably get a great education while bonding together over an interesting topic.

You'd be surprised how many people are willing to spend time with total strangers talking about what they do and what they love (hopefully, they're one and the same). I've found that business professionals are especially open to talking with young people who show a legitimate interest in their subject.

Two pieces of advice: First, you can show the person you're meeting with some respect by studying a little about the field they're in and putting together some intelligent questions in advance; don't just walk in off the street, slouch down in a seat, and take a "tell me what you know" attitude. Second, always remember to send a thank-you note after your meeting. Remember, these people are taking time out of their busy day to do a favor for you; you should at least prepare for the meeting, be respectful and polite, and thank the person for their time afterward.

Create "Homework" Assignments

This is similar to field trips, the main difference being that homework assignments should end with a tangible product. This could be something as simple as having your son write a short report on what he learned from one of your field trip meetings (you, the parent, could also write a report, and then compare your findings with those of your son's), or a task such as opening a savings account together, researching a stock or mutual fund and making an investment together, or balancing your checkbook together each month.

Match Funds

You could consider encouraging your teen to save or invest by matching funds up to a certain amount. For example, you could agree that any money your teen raised for investing or saving for a minimum of one year would get matching funds of up to five hundred dollars from you. Parents get pleasure from giving things to their kids, but giving money to match a teen's own hard-earned savings can be a more constructive approach than just buying them an expensive gift.

Encourage Your Teen

Yes, I said it earlier, but it's so important that it's worth repeating: if your teen is interested in something like setting up his or her own business or learning more about money, you should consider yourself very lucky and do anything possible to nurture this interest.

Be positive, be creative, be active, and be involved.

Appendix: The full business plan for Healthy Parties for Kids, LLC ("HPK")

Executive Summary

Twenty-five percent of children between the ages of six and twelve in this country are obese, and the rate of childhood diabetes has more than doubled in the last twenty years. Parents want their kids to eat healthy foods and get outside to play, but often throw these values out the window during special occasions like birthday parties.

Healthy Parties for Kids, LLC ("HPK"), was set up to plan and deliver nutritional party alternatives to young people. Our mission is to improve the health of children and ease the burdens of busy parents by organizing and hosting healthy and enjoyable gatherings for children.

We offer fun and healthy parties and events for people between the ages of one and 14.

The children's birthday party market in the U.S. is estimated to be a $10 billion industry that should grow to over $20 billion in the next five years. We target families with a median income of $75,000 near the downtown area, and estimate that there are over 50,000 kids in our target market.

HPK provides convenience and peace of mind for parents, while entertaining their children with fun, active games and providing them with nutritious, enjoyable foods and drinks.

In less than ten minutes, parents can choose from a set of party options on our web site, selecting from a variety of budgets, activities, and themes. A few clicks and it's done: HPK takes over, mailing invitations and thank-you cards, buying and preparing treats, setting up and taking down decorations, leading kids through games and events, and explaining the importance of making nutrition and physical fitness a part of their everyday lives. Parents can rest easy knowing that the organization and management of their child's important day are in good hands. Mom and Dad can spend their time enjoying the day and creating memories with their children.

Competition for our company is sparse, with only a small number of companies focusing on parties for young people. A typical birthday party at one of our competitors runs $425 on average, but parents complain about the "rush and routine" at these places. Aside from our basic, healthy-party approach, HPK has many advantages over our competitors:

- **We are affordable**—about 20 percent cheaper than our average competitor.
- **We are flexible**—we can accommodate many dates and times.
- **We are familiar**—we are members of the community and have worked with many kids and their parents.
- **We are local**—we are not a chain with a "one-size-fits all" approach to events.
- **We are timely**—we address a pressing need in the market, at a critical time.

Our company provides affordable, safe, and fun parties for kids, with special attention devoted to each party and child. We offer a range of healthy foods and fun activities, and our staff engages with the children, using their names, talking about their favorite characters, and giving them quality time and attention. Most parties are held at the parents' home or in public parks, and we encourage outdoor play and activity. With four founders and a large group of responsible and trained friends and helpers, we are able to offer up to three different parties in three locations at any given date and time, meaning that three kids with the same birthday can each be accommodated.

Our business was formed and is run by four high school friends. We have years of experience in dealing with children through our babysitting jobs, and have tested the kid party planning concept for over six months. We are ready to launch in the beginning of May, and will be fully functional by the start of school summer vacation, a key time for children's outdoor birthday parties. We are seeking an additional investment or loan of $3,000 to purchase business supplies and a vehicle. We believe that HPK can grow to $300,000 of sales and $60,000 of profits within five years of start-up.

Going forward, we anticipate opportunities to expand the business into teen and corporate parties and events, form a partnership with a local food company that would allow us to create our own brand of pre-made healthy entrees for kids, and franchise the business nationwide. The founders expect to run the business indefinitely, working while in college and after graduation.

Nature of the Business

Healthy Parties for Kids ("HPK") is dedicated to offering fun and healthy parties for children between one and fourteen years old. Our target market is parents with kids in this age group, living within a 15-mile radius of downtown, and with a median income level of $75,000. We estimate that there are over 50,000 people who fit this description in our target age group and geography. To us, this means 50,000 opportunities to change the idea of what a birthday party is and what it can offer.

HPK's owners conducted surveys of nearly 100 parents that used our competitors' services for their child's party and found that the following four things were the key decision criteria; they are, therefore, what we believe are the critical success factors for our business:

- **Affordability:** Parents are willing to spend between
- $15 and $20 per child for a three-hour party.
- **Availability:** It's important that a weekend date near a child's birthday or big event is available.
- **Familiarity:** Parents know what to expect from a party at our established competitors; they have peace of mind knowing that staff are experienced in dealing with kids.
- **Safety and fun:** It is important that the party be held in a safe place, with safe activities, but also that the kids be entertained and enjoy themselves.

Parents indicated that the main things they didn't like about parties at our competitors' were the following:

- **Routine and rush:** Parents feel that their kids are often "rushed out" of a party space in order to make way for the next party, and that there's no individual attention. ("It feels like a party factory, and no one knows or really cares about my kid.")
- **Limited range of food and activities:** Over half of all parents surveyed said that they were fed up with "another pizza and cake" party, or parties in which their kids had access to video games or simply ran around an indoor play area (something they felt wasn't unique or "particularly special").

Our company provides affordable, safe, and fun parties for kids, with special attention devoted to each party and child. We offer a range of healthy foods and fun activities, and our staff engages with the children, using their names, talking about their favorite characters, and giving them quality time and attention. Most parties are held at the parents' home or in public parks, and we encourage outdoor play and activity.

With four founders and a large group of responsible and trained staff and helpers, we are able to offer up to three different parties in three locations at any given date and time, meaning that three kids with the same birthday, wanting parties around lunchtime can all be accommodated—something our competitors, Boingo Gym and Charlie Cheese, can't accommodate and don't manage well (three parties in the same large room means a chaotic mess of kids from different parties "getting lost" in the crowds).

In summary, our competitive advantages are as follows:

- **We are affordable**—nearly twenty percent cheaper than the average competitor.
- **We can accommodate many dates and times**—up to three different parties in three different locations, meaning no "jumble" of kids in one single space.
- **We are familiar**—all of the founders and most of the helpers are students in the local high school. We babysit for the children, and many of their parents already know and trust us.
- **We offer safe and fun parties**, with a variety of games, activities, and treats.
- **We are not a chain**, but local members of the community that see the kids we entertain in our neighborhoods and communities. We have ties to the community that a franchised business cannot develop.
- **We emphasize customer service and attention**—we know many of the kids we arrange parties for, and we treat each child as unique and special, making particular

efforts to use their name and know their age and other things about them.

- **<u>We address a pressing need in the market, at a key time</u>**. Parents are increasingly concerned about the junk food diets that many kids have access to, and are searching for alternatives. We provide a solution to this problem and answer to the concerns.

Company Goals

Immediate (next one to four weeks):

- Complete business plan and approach bank for a business loan

- Register company with secretary of state

- Obtain EIN and set up bank accounts

Near-Term (next three to six months):

- Create promotional material and distribute at "Springfield Kids Fair" in January

- Sign up 25 new customers

- Finish web site creation and testing

Mid-Term (next 12-24 months):

- Obtain bank or other loan to purchase delivery truck

- Sign partnership agreement with health food company for cross-promotion and joint purchasing

- Begin expansion into teen- and corporate-party business areas

Long-Term (three to five years):

- Generate 25 percent of revenues from non-children's parties
- Begin expansion into "pre-made" healthy meal segment (HPK makes healthy meals for kids, and strategic partner sells in their stores)
- Begin process of franchising the business

Details of the Company

Registered Name:
Healthy Parties for Kids, LLC

Date of Formation:
January 1

Company Legal Form:
Delaware Limited Liability Corporation

Company Ownership and Paid-In Capital:
Trinity Adams, President, 20%, $500
Jordan Logus, Director of Sales and Marketing, 20%, $500
Ariel Miller, Director of Operations, 20%, $500
Bailey Lee, Director of Finance, 20%, $500
Other Paid-In Capital, 20%, $1,000

Company Mission Statement and Vision:
Healthy Parties for Kids is dedicated to improving the health of children and easing the burdens of busy parents by organizing and hosting healthy and enjoyable gatherings for young people.

Key Milestones Achieved To Date:

- Market study and competitive analysis

- Customer Needs survey of over 100 parents

- Organization of over a dozen events for target audience

- Revenue of over $4,000 in the past six months

- Drafting of business plan

- Formation of LLC

- Creation of web site with Twitter feed and "birthday blog"

Market Analysis

Industry Size, Growth, and Trends

In the last 50 years, a typical eight-year-old's birthday party has changed from a gathering of five to ten friends at the child's home, with a few games (Pin the Tail on the Donkey, Twister) and cake being served, to large and elaborate gatherings of 100 people or more, with paid entertainers, bouncy houses, ponies, and a variety of themes. The increase in single-parent households and households in which both parents work has created a need for convenience, as many moms and dads today do not have the time to plan and run a party for their children, yet remain committed to the idea of giving their young ones a memorable event.

Background data on our industry is very favorable for HPK:

- The children's birthday party market in the U.S. is estimated to be a $10 billion industry, and one that has grown by over 10 percent a year over the last decade. (Author's note: all of this data is fictional; when you do cite statistics and data, you will need to cite sources of those.)

- Billings Research estimates that the kid's party industry will grow to over $20 billion in the next five years, as busy parents increasingly "outsource" the planning and hosting of children's parties to outside vendors.

- The average outside party cost for a child has risen from less than $100 ten years ago to over $250 currently, according to Vector Party Research.

- There was no noticeable decline in party spending for kids during the economic recession of 2007–2008.

- Demographics are favorable, with nearly 20 million people moving into our target market over the next three years.

The Local Industry and Competitors

- There are 17 party planners in the city, but none focus on young kids.

- There are three established companies that regularly host parties for kids.

- Competitors' costs are higher than HPK's, capacity is limited, and many parents are tired of their "routine."

Our research finds 17 companies that are active in party arrangement in our city. None of these companies focuses exclusively on children, and over half are geared toward weddings and office parties.

Three companies that do regularly host birthday parties for children in our area—Charlie Cheese Pizza, Boingo Gym, and Carl's Bowling and Arcade—do a brisk business. Our observations over a two-month period indicate an average of seven parties a day on Saturday and Sunday, with average attendance of fourteen people and an average total price of $425, for an average per weekend revenue of nearly $6,000 per location.

Discussions with managers at these businesses reveal that the birthday business has grown between 20 and 30 percent for each business in the last two years, and is expected to continue growing at a similar rate for the foreseeable future.

Our Target Market

- Parents with children between one and fourteen years old

- Families within a 15-mile radius of downtown

- Relatively affluent, with median income of $75,000 per household

- Approximately 50,000 kids in our target market

- New market opportunity: Many parents choose to have parties at home because they don't appreciate the junk food and cookie-cutter nature of parties at other locations; we can tap this market of health-and-fitness-conscious parents who "want something different" in their child's birthday party.

Our Positioning and Competitive Advantage

HPK's owners conducted surveys of nearly 100 parents that used our competitors' services for their child's party and found that the following four things were the key decision criteria and what we believe are the critical success factors:

- <u>Affordability:</u> Parents are willing to spend between $15 and $20 per child for a three-hour party.
- <u>Availability:</u> It's important that a weekend date near a child's birthday or big event is available.
- <u>Familiarity:</u> Parents know what to expect from a party at our established competitors; they have peace of mind knowing that staff are experienced in dealing with kids.

- <u>Safety and fun:</u> It is important that the party be held in a safe place, with safe activities, but also that the kids be entertained and enjoy themselves.

Competitive Positioning:

	HPK	Charlie Cheese	Boingo Gym	Adam's Arcade
"Basic Package" Average Cost (20 kids, 10 parents)	$ 350.00	$ 435.00	$ 425.00	$ 405.00
Cost of Facilities, food & other	Included	$ 385.00	$ 375.00	$ 355.00
Cost of cake, invitations & other	Included	$ 50.00	$ 50.00	$ 50.00
# of parties that can be held at one time	3	5	1	2
# of Themes Available	5	1	1	1
# of Activities Available	37	1	2	2
# of Menu Items	75	8	4	15

	HPK	Charlie Cheese
Average Party Cost	$ 350.0	$ 435.0
Cost of Facilities, food, etc	Included	$ 385.0
Cost of cake, invitations, etc	Included	$ 50.0
# of parties that can be held	3	5
# of Themes	5	1
# of Activities	37	1 (arcade)
# of Menu Items	75	8
Familiarity	Founders and employees are members of community and babysit for parents	Well-known national brand
Strengths	Affordable, safe, convenient, unique, healthy, personal attention to kids, health & fitness appeal	Brand, predictability, can hold many parties simultaneously
Weaknesses	Lack of brand awareness	Chaotic Unhealthy Kids get little personal attention
Opportunities	Appeal to people that throw own parties because they can't afford or don't like the "corporate" party feel Easy to expand -- large labor pool; easy to train new hires	
Threats	Low barriers to entry	

Prior to launching the business, the four founders organized and ran over a dozen birthday parties with a total of over 250 attendees. Feedback was very positive in every event, and testimonials can be found in the appendix, along with sample marketing materials (fliers and a snapshot of our web page), and a menu of different party options (themes, activities, treats, etc.).

Other Opportunities, Purchase Patterns, and Market Access

- There is a large potential market of parents who host their own parties because they want the party to be at home, don't like "corporate" kid's parties, and want their kids to have more individual attention. Our competitors cannot tap this market.

- We could potentially expand to healthy office parties, corporate events, and high school events (i.e., dances, parties).

- Birthdays occur only once a year, but parents who choose to use a competitor like Charlie Cheese one year aren't likely to return the next year (they want to provide a variety of experiences for their child); HPK can expect significant repeat business, as our parties are distinct from one another and customizable (two parents that we hosted parties with during our "trial period" have already asked us to organize parties for their other kids).

- We have good access to the market through community, church, and school involvement. We have a network of kids we regularly babysit for, and plan to send public relations letters to local newspapers and television news. We run a blog about our parties and have over 4,000 followers on our Twitter networks.

Organization and Team

Our business was formed and is run by four high school friends who have grown up together. We have years of experience in dealing with children through our babysitting jobs, and have tested the kid party planning idea for over six months.

Executives and Key Personnel

The founders and key members of the Company are as follows:

Trinity Adams, President

Trinity is a senior at Springfield High School. She is the student body vice president, a cheerleader, and a member of the honor society. Trinity spent two years working for Daddy Day Care of Springfield, helping to organize teaching curriculum, ordering supplies and equipment, making meals, and working with other staff. She has been a babysitter in the community for nearly five years, and a volunteer with Habitat for Humanity for two years. Trinity sets the strategic direction of the Company, and is involved in all key aspects of decision-making.

Jordan Logas, Director of Sales and Marketing

Jordan became interested in sales and marketing three years ago when she started working with Big Jim's Catering, helping the owner identify and sign new catering clients. Jordan has helped local businesses create and manage web sites to advertise their services, and has advised two companies on Internet marketing strategies. She is a senior at Springfield High School.

Ariel Miller, Director of Operations

Ariel has spent three years working at Salad Express, where she is an assistant manager. She has experience with supplier relations, inventory control, deliveries and catering, cooking procedures, and employee management. She is a senior at Springfield High School, and a member of the Cooking Club.

Bailey Lee, Director of Accounting and Finance

Bailey is a junior at Springfield High School, where she serves as class treasurer and is a member of the Business Club. Her interest in accounting and finance came from her parents, who run a small business and have taught her the basics of bookkeeping, accounting, and finance. She has worked on the financials of the family business, a coffee shop and deli, for the past four years.

Kelly Lee, Business Advisor

Kelly, Bailey's mother, is an accomplished businesswoman who has set up and run two successful food-service businesses, Kelly's Bagels and Kelly's Coffee & Cake, both of Springfield. Kelly advises the Company on key management and operational issues. She is a member of the Springfield Restaurant Association, Springfield Chamber of Commerce, Springfield School Board, and Springfield Community Church. She won the coveted "Best Businesswoman" award from the Springfield Chamber of Commerce in 2004.

Relationship Between the Founders

The founders of the company grew up together in Springfield, attending elementary, junior high, and high school together. They have a strong and long-lasting friendship, and have worked together in other business ventures (a babysitting business). The founders have complementary skills and talents, and work well together.

The Ownership of the Company:

Ownership of the Company is as follows:

Name	Role	Paid-In Capital	% Ownership
Trinity Adams	Co-Founder	$ 500.00	20.0%
Jordan Logas	Co-Founder	$ 500.00	20.0%
Ariel Miller	Co-Founder	$ 500.00	20.0%
Bailey Lee	Co-Founder	$ 500.00	20.0%
Kelly Lee	Advisor	$ 500.00	15.0%
Kyle Lee	Investor	$ 500.00	5.0%
Total		$ 3,000.00	100.0%

The Future of the Team

All of the team members plan to remain in Springfield following their graduation from high school, allowing us to continue working together to grow our business after graduation.

The résumés of all founders can be found in the Appendixes.

Operations Strategy

Marketing and Sales Strategy:

HPK has a multifaceted approach to marketing our services:

- **Web-based marketing:** The Company has a web site that allows customers to get information on our services, read testimonials from satisfied customers, print coupons, and get more information. We use AdWords on Google, have 20,000 followers on Twitter, and have a blog. We are well reviewed on Yelp.
- **Word of mouth and referral:** Anyone who refers us to a person that becomes a customer receives a $20 savings bond in their child's name. We offer a 10 percent discount on any repeat business.

- **Print advertising:** The Company has posted fliers on the bulletin boards of the YMCA, area churches, the library, and other places where parents with young children assemble. We are speaking with the PTAs of two elementary schools about distributing information to their members. In the future, the company anticipates advertising in *Springfield Parents Magazine*.
- **PR:** The Company has a public relations strategy, mailing press releases to local newspapers and television news stations (see Appendix).
- **Other:** The Company is negotiating with a local health food store about the prospect of the store "sponsoring" our business—providing food and drinks to the Company at heavily discounted prices in return for our company advertising the store at our events and on our web site.

Personnel Plan:

The Company regularly hires high school students the founders know to assist on an "as-needed" basis, with hourly pay levels of $10.00-15.00. The average party requires only one to two people to plan, host, and clean up, so personnel in addition to the four managers are only required if more than two parties are being held at the same time on a given date. In every case, our Company has a minimum of two weeks, and an average of four weeks, advance notice about the details of the party—ample time to source additional personnel, if necessary.

Growth Strategy

HPK anticipates handling an average of 10 parties a week by the end of one year of operations. By the end of the first year, we anticipate hiring and training two to three additional employees, and increasing the offering of products, branching into teen events (Sweet 16 parties, proms) and corporate events (store openings, office parties). In the long term, we believe there is the potential to franchise the business.

Funding Request

HPK is seeking $6,000 in capital to fund equipment and inventory purchases. Owners and their family members will contribute $3,000 from personal savings, while the Company is seeking an additional $3,000 in the form of a bank loan.

The main uses of money raised will be the purchase of a used utility van to allow the Company to deliver materials to parties (the Company currently uses a friend's pickup truck, but the availability of that vehicle cannot be guaranteed), the purchase of inventory and equipment, and fees paid to our website developer to enhance the Company's on-line presence.

The Source and Use of Funds Statement is as follows:

Source of Funds	Amount	Use of Funds	Amount
Owner Capital	$ 3,000.00	Website enhancement costs	$ 1,000.00
(see "Ownership Section" of the business plan)		Marketing materials	$ 1,500.00
Bank Loan	$ 3,000.00	Used van for delivery	$ 3,500.00
Total Sources	**$ 6,000.00**	**Total Uses**	**$ 6,000.00**

The Company believes that it will not need to seek additional capital for the foreseeable future, as the business is expected to be cash flow positive from its third month, as detailed in the Financials Section of this Business Plan.

Risks

HPK believes there are three main risks associated with our business:

1. **Weather:** Most of the Company's parties are held outdoors, either in the host family's yard or at reserved sites in public

parks. Customers typically book their parties four to six weeks in advance, but the Company offers a 50 percent refund if the event is cancelled due to inclement weather. There is a risk that poor weather can substantially lower the amount of revenue the Company is able to earn. Management has been working on new indoor party themes and venues that could serve as "backup plans", allowing the Company to receive full payment even in the event of poor weather.

2. **Equipment:** The Company relies upon the use of large delivery vehicles (a pickup truck and trailer) that may not be available to the Company at all times. The Company is discussing a vehicle loan from a credit union, and may be able to purchase a truck for business use within six months.

3. **Economic Risk:** Children's parties are discretionary, high-ticket events. Economic weakness could lead more parents to organize parties on their own, or opt for lower-priced alternatives to hosted parties. The Company is working on creating a range of lower-cost party options to address this risk.

Future Strategy and Exit

The Company believes it will continue growing beyond the involvement of the four original founders, and has crafted a growth strategy that addresses the changes in management that we anticipate.

Three of the four founding partners of HPK are beginning their senior year in high school, while the fourth partner is beginning her junior year. Next year, it is possible that one of the founding partners, Trinity, will move out of state for college, but three of the other founders will remain in Springfield. Jordan is likely to attend Springfield University, but plans to continue working part-time for the Company. Ariel plans to work full-time for the Company after high school. Bailey will continue working part-time during the school year and full-time during weekends and holidays.

The founders of the Company plan to hire a professional manager within nine months of start-up. This manager will work closely with the founders, learning the business and helping to implement new growth strategies, such as organizing parties for teens, corporate clients, and others.

Although management anticipates operating the Company for the foreseeable future, discussions with a business broker in Springfield indicate that a business of our nature with strong growth prospects (20 percent net profit growth per year for at least five years) should be able to sell for 1.25–1.5 times annual revenues. We estimate revenues in Year Five of our business to be $300,000, indicating a potential exit value of $375,000 to $450,000 at that time, should an exit be sought.

Appendixes

Appendix 1: HPK marketing materials and fliers

Appendix 2: Testimonials, reviews, and surveys

Appendix 3: Party options menu, pricing list, and other products

Appendix 4: Detailed financial statements and key financial assumptions